THE LAST SCENES
OF THE ODYSSEY

MNEMOSYNE

BIBLIOTHECA CLASSICA BATAVA

COLLEGERUNT

W. DEN BOER · W. J. VERDENIUS · R. E. H. WESTENDORP BOERMA

BIBLIOTHECAE FASCICULOS EDENDOS CURAVIT

W. J. VERDENIUS, HOMERUSLAAN 53, ZEIST

SUPPLEMENTUM QUINQUAGESIMUM SECUNDUM

DOROTHEA WENDER

THE LAST SCENES
OF THE ODYSSEY

LUGDUNI BATAVORUM E. J. BRILL MCMLXXVIII

THE LAST SCENES OF THE ODYSSEY

BY

DOROTHEA WENDER

LUGDUNI BATAVORUM E. J. BRILL MCMLXXVIII

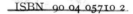

ISBN 90 04 05710 2

For John H. Finley, Jr.

CONTENTS

ACKNOWLEDGEMENTS

Jennifer Roberts, my friend and colleague in the Wheaton College classics department, has been unfailingly helpful and encouraging. Sharon Jackiw, of the German department, gave me some indispensable assistance, and I am grateful to her, too. I want to thank Nancy Shepardson, Alice Peterson and their able assistants, for their skill and cheerfulness in preparing the manuscript. Finally, I am grateful to Wheaton College, and in particular the excellent library staff, for essential assistance. This is a good place to work.

I. INTRODUCTION

"Some on the leaves of ancient authors prey,
Nor time nor moths e'er spoiled so much as they."
—Pope, *Essay on Criticism*

Odysseus and Penelope have finally retired to bed. They converse. She talks about the suitors; he—the night having been lengthened conveniently—recounts the bulk of the *Odyssey*. Dawn comes, and the hero sets out for his father's farm. Hermes, meanwhile, is leading the shades of the suitors to the house of Hades. There the ghosts meet Achilles and Agamemnon, and summarize for the Achaean heroes those books of the epic not already retold by Odysseus. Back in Ithaca, Odysseus makes himself known to the aged Laertes. The kinsmen of the dead suitors assemble, desiring revenge, but Zeus and Athene have decided for peace. So, after a brief skirmish, the antagonists are reconciled, and the story comes to an end.

This conclusion of the *Odyssey*, the only one we have, has been under attack for twenty-three centuries. Critics, both Unitarian and Analyst, have used every type of argument against it; linguistic evidence, they say, brands the book (that is, the entire section, Book xxiii, 297 to xxiv, 548) as late; the culture and theology of xxiv is inconsistent with "Homeric" usage; the great Alexandrians tell us the poem concludes with xxiii, 296; and, of course, the end of the *Odyssey* is incompetently written: boring, awkward, and superfluous.

There *is* a disappointing flatness about the very last scene. Even most of us who think the conclusion genuine would admit that the very end is rather abrupt and perfunctory. Still, I am sure that the whole conclusion is Homeric—that is, was composed by the same poet who composed the rest of the *Odyssey*—and it is my purpose in this study to impart that same conviction, as far as possible, to my readers.

It's a formidable job. The case against the Conclusion looks terrifyingly strong, particularly to anyone who falls under the spell of the many-wiled Page, whose ability to denigrate, castigate, and vilify—now with a stiletto, now with a poleax—has surely not been matched since Housman. The timid dragon who fears to do battle with Sir Denys, however, should bear in mind, first, that much of what looks serious in his work is really written for fun, in a pure spirit of innocent merriment,[1] and second, that points which seem unanswerable in his argument can often be answered after all, or even sometimes annihilated. Still, it may occasionally appear that my entire study is directed almost exclusively to a personal attack on this one scholar. That is not really the case; if I often single out remarks of Page for disagreement, it is because his is the most vigorous and comprehensive of the modern attacks on the Conclusion, and he is a worthy and articulate πρόμαχος for the rest of the attacking forces.

I am not the first to try to rescue the *Odyssey* Conclusion from its attackers. Over against Casaubon, Spohn, Wilamowitz, Allen, Monroe, Murray, Kirk, Bowra and Page (to mention only a few) are found Alexander Pope, Lang, Scott, Bassett, Carpenter, Van der Valk, Shewan, Woodhouse, Whitman, Armstrong, Lord, Shephard, and Erbse. But few of the prosecutors and few of the defenders have attempted to examine all the evidence both for and against the Conclusion.

Neither the defense nor the prosecution lacks evidence. The major problem is that the evidence is of different kinds. While the critics rely chiefly on the presence in Book xxiv of linguistic and cultural material which is apparently alien to Homeric usage, the supporters rely mainly on evidence that xxiv is structurally necessary to the *Odyssey* and seems to be in harmony with the intentions and attitudes of the rest of the poem. While the critics' evidence is composed chiefly of external, that is, linguistic and archaeological data, the defenders' data are mainly internal, or literary. "Literary", however, should not here mean subjective, purely aesthetic; the literary data used by the defense are presumed to be no less factual than those of the prosecution, and should give the prosecutors as much trouble as the prosecutors' own data give to the defenders. For example, there are several passages in the *Odyssey* which lead the reader to expect an eventual reunion of Odysseus with his old

---

[1] That Sir Denys's style is intended as *humor* can be readily seen in *The Homeric Odyssey* (p. 17), where he says "Let us avoid extremes; a mind free from prejudice—", or page 52, "Let us inquire into the matter, preserving so far as possible that patience and good humor which—" Coming from Sir Denys, these phrases rival the death of Little Nell in their ability to provoke mirth.

father. The real purpose of these passages may be a matter for argument, their genuineness may also be disputed, but the presence of those passages in our manuscripts is a *fact*, one of the data relied on by the defense. Purely aesthetic judgments, on the other hand, should have little place on either side of the argument, although both sides do in fact make considerable use of value judgment. Such judgments cannot be considered as evidence; they are the handmaidens of Peitho, and with equal justice Spohn can call the second Nekuia "impedientem et audientium exspectationi molestam" and Woodhouse can describe precisely the same scene as "one of Homer's greatest strokes."

This is the plan of the study: in the next chapter, I will discuss, rather briefly, some recent scholarly work on what the Germans, so aptly, call "die *Oral Poetry*," and will examine the bearing of that work on our question. Then, I will examine in turn each part of the Conclusion to the *Odyssey*—which falls, neatly, into four parts. In my discussion of the first part, I will try to demonstrate that the opinion of the Alexandrian critics is more or less irrelevant, and further, that the *Odyssey* could not have ended at any of the likely stopping-places in Book xxiii. In the following two chapters, I will discuss the Underworld scene and Homeric conceptions about death and the afterlife. I trust that in these chapters I shall firmly lay to rest a number of insubstantial phantoms: for example the idea that in Homer an unburied person's shade can never enter the underworld, and that Hermes has no business there, either. I find the second Nekuia not only perfectly consistent with Homeric "theology," but necessary, in several ways, to the literary unity of the Odyssey. My discussion of the Laertes episode is concerned largely with linguistic matters and the problem of Dolius. Finally, in my treatment of the battle scene, I discuss, among other things, why the last scene, with its emphasis on fathers and sons, is necessary and appropriate to the theme of the whole poem.

I hope, of course, that all my readers will be convinced, after reading my arguments, that the Conclusion of the *Odyssey* is genuine. However, it is just possible (I admit) that some shadows of doubt may linger. For those readers who remain—even after all my arguments—skeptical, I offer a neat package of plausible historical hypotheses, which may help to explain how the ending of the *Odyssey* came to be, as it is, a not entirely satisfying conclusion to the poem. I have bundled these historical conjectures into

an appendix, on page 76. I should say at this point that all my
historical hypotheses assume unity of authorship for the rest of the
Odyssey. This study will make the same assumption. I shall try,
however, to avoid getting into the question of whether or not the
Iliad was composed by the same man who composed the *Odyssey*,
by a different man, by a woman, or by a divinely inspired com-
mittee, and whether or not his, her, their, name was Homer. When
I say "Homer," I shall mean the author of the *Odyssey*. One exception: where criticisms of xxiv are based on supposed "Homeric"
usage, on the function of Hermes, for example, I will use both
epics as evidence for what Homeric usage is. One further exception:
I shall attempt to demonstrate that a major feature of the *Odyssey*
is its criticism of the Iliad, its author's deliberate revision of the
Iliadic definitions of virtue and the heroic. In the *Odyssey*, Odysseus
is seen as superior to Achilles (and to Agamemnon) because he
succeeds, has the sort of polytropous flexibility of character which
allows success, and the domesticity which makes success worth
having. The author of the *Odyssey* does not admire a splendid,
one-sided failure, as the author of the *Iliad*, perhaps, does. This
statement does not mean that I assume the poems were composed
by different poets; I assume that many years passed between the
composition of the *Iliad* and that of the *Odyssey*, and time and
experience have been known to change poets as well as lesser
mortals.

  With regard to the evidence against the *Odyssey* conclusion—the
case for the prosecution—my course is clear; I shall try to mini-
mize, explain, or destroy every possible objection to the Conclusion.
With regard to the positive, "literary" evidence, I hope to demonstrate that the Conclusion enriches the whole poem and casts
brilliant light on what Homer was trying to say in his great epic.

II. ON ORAL AND OTHER MATTERS

Fashions in the world of Homeric scholarship change as un-predictably and erratically as do those in women's wear. It is hard at any time to make an authoritative statement like "The Unitarians have won", or "No-one now doubts the oral nature of Homeric poetry", since at the very same moment, Yale may be moving away from some widely held doctrine while Harvard stays loyally with it, while Leipzig continues to reject it, and Framingham State has not yet heard of it. In the decade in which Frederick Combellack was telling us that the Unitarians had conquered,[1] at least one midwestern university was telling its graduate students that there had been only one serious unitarian, John Scott, a fanatic, and since he was dead the cause had died.

Still, I would guess, very tentatively, that at this date a majority of living Homeric scholars are or have become more or less unitarian, and also, that they believe that Homer (or two Homers at most) was an illiterate oral poet.

Recently, however, the doctrine of Homer as oral poet has been challenged.[2] There has been a growing, perhaps inevitable reaction against what M. W. M. Pope has called the "new orthodoxy" of Homer as oral poet.[3]

There has been a steady chipping away at the foundations of oral theory, so that none of those foundations seem so solid as before. Douglas Young has been disapproved of for the unseemliness of his polemic tone, by some scholars who are perhaps not aware that for many others the battle scenes are half the fun of Homeric scholarship. (Such critics would probably have advised Juvenal to tone down his language and avoid sweeping generalizations.) At any rate, Young has presented us with some important data, which are highly relevant to the study of oral poetry. For example, there have been oral poets (like Duncan Macintyre) who dispensed with

---

[1] F. M. Combellack, "Contemporary Unitarians and Homeric Originality", *AJP* LXXI, 4 (1950), p. 337.

[2] Much of the material in this chapter appears in slightly different form in my article "Homer, Avdo Međedović, and 'The Elephant's Child' ". AJP 98 (1977), 327-347.

[3] "The Parry-Lord Theory of Homeric Composition", *Acta Classica* 6 (1964), a stimulating essay on the dogmatism of oral theory.

formulaic language altogether; there have also been many literate poets who used it deliberately, like Cynewulf. There *are* "transitional" works. Some writers compose easily, almost without "blotting a line"; others require much premeditation and revision.

Before his untimely death, Adam Parry was beginning to question the implications of his father's great work; this apparent lapse from filial piety was also supported by Anne Amory Parry. George Dimock's fine article "From Homer to Novi Pazar and Back" argues convincingly, I think, that metrical correctness is no problem for the oral poet, who can think in meter, and that formulas and formulaic expressions are used deliberately (by both oral and literary poets) because they are poetic, not because they help out the improviser.[4] I have tried, in a recent article, to confirm Dimock's suggestions and carry them a bit further by positing that formulas are characteristic of works composed for oral *performance*, not necessarily by illiterate composers. For example, Kipling's prose story, "The Elephant's Child", contains a higher percentage of formulas than does the *Iliad*.

Thus the "rules" of oral theory, which seemed so secure in the writings of Parry, Lord, and Notopoulos, all seem to have important exceptions. There is still, I think, general agreement that the Homeric poems were not created *ex nihilo*, and that they rest on a long tradition of (probably) oral poetry. The length of the Homeric poems has always been a problem; *The Wedding of Smailagić Meho* has now demonstrated to my satisfaction that length is *not* such a problem. By analogy with *Meho*, I do not now find it hard to conceive of an oral poet with Homer's abilities creating an *Iliad* or an *Odyssey* without a written outline or a text to refer to.[5] In

---

[4] George Dimock, "From Homer to Novi Pazar and Back", *Arion* 2, no. 14 (1963), pp. 40-57.

[5] *Why* he would want to is still a problem, and the Yugoslav analogy is not at all helpful. Lord (SINGER) tells us that the ends of the (short) tales of the guslars are often not performed, because the audience tends to get bored and leave the coffeehouse. Even the great Avdo had a problem finding an audience for his longer productions: (MEHO 298) (in 1950) Avdo . . . "said that he had not sung the song since 1935, because there was no one with a deep enough interest (meraklija) to listen." He had clearly put out a special effort for the American professor. In fact, despite Lord's assertions (SINGER and elsewhere) that the oral poet has no interest in having his work preserved, Avdo said that he wanted his *Meho* of 1950 to be less good than the 1935 version, because the older one *had been translated into English*. (298) Perhaps Avdo was not such a despiser of *kleos* after all!

other words, it seems *possible* that an *Odyssey* could be orally composed, by a genius. But does *Meho* prove that the *Odyssey* actually *was* so composed? It does not. To be sure, the differences between *Meho* and the *Odyssey* could all be explained by a difference in the talent of the poets. But the similarities can not be explained *only* by assuming that both are orally composed poems, for every one of these traits (including the high percentage of formulas) can be found also in works we know to have been written. I do suspect, as I have said, that some of the similarities stem from both works' having been composed for oral performance, but I must admit that this cannot be proved, either, since some "oral sounding" works (the *Iliad*, for example) are popular with readers as well as with hearers, and some "literary-sounding" works (Herodotus, for example) have been composed for oral performance.

Transmission remains the major problem. It does not seem likely (pace Kirk) that the Homeric poems were orally transmitted. There are, apparently, no longer objections to the idea that writing was known in Homer's day. Lord has insisted on dictation as the answer [6] because in *his* experience literate oral poets are not as good (as poets) as illiterate ones. But his numbers are, after all, small, and he has a tendency to extrapolate rather extravagantly. For example, on the basis of two blind guslars that he encountered, he generalizes that blind poets are not usually very good.[7] The implied corollary is "therefore Homer was not blind." Well, perhaps he was, and perhaps he wasn't, but Lord's two blind guslars will never give us the answer, and two or 20 or 200 bad literate guslars will never prove that Homer was illiterate. There *are* Yugoslav poets (whether bad or good) who write down the poems they have composed in their heads. "The Song of Milman Parry", by Milovan Vojičić, was written in this way: Lord calls it an "autograph oral" poem.[8] But isn't this precisely the way Virgil composed, and Milton, and T. S. Eliot? We *all* compose "orally", in this sense; many of us even leave the desk and pace around the room when we want to get the phrasing just right. Then we write it down. There is obviously a great difference between composing orally

---

[6] In "Homer's Originality: Oral Dictated Texts", *TAPA* 84 (1953), pp. 124-34, also in Kirk, *Language* etc.(book of readings cited in note 20), and elsewhere.

[7] Lord, *The Singer of Tales* (Cambridge, Mass., 1960), p. 18.

[8] *Ibid.*, pp. 129 and 272-5.

during a performance, and writing in privacy as slowly as one wishes. But the difference between composing orally for an amanuensis and composing orally for *oneself* as amanuensis seems to me minimal—and by the law of Occam's Razor we should, parsimoniously, incline more toward a literate (or "orally autographic") Homer, than toward the combination of an illiterate but talented Homer and an untalented but literate secretary whose motives were indeed obscure.

I have come to believe that Homer was literate, and that the "oral" features in Homer—the formulas, epithets, catalogues, and repeated passages—are there not out of necessity, but for positive effect. These features no doubt arose during a long tradition of oral poetry, to which they are appropriate, but they did not die out instantly, the moment poets began to compose in writing. The case of Hesiod is even clearer, I think: as M. L. West says,[9] it is hard to imagine generations of poets carefully memorizing and reciting and passing on to their successors lines like "Perses, let's settle our argument here and now", and "I have been on a ship only once, when I went to the games of Amphidamas and won a tripod."

And yet "oral" features clearly are present in Hesiod, as in Homer. Even if these two (or three or four) poets *were* literate, the work of Parry and the Yugoslav analogies are still useful to the Homeric scholar, for they help us to see that some features in Homer—the long, tedious, slightly irrelevant catalogue, for example, or the doublet episode—are not blunders but regular features of traditional heroic song.[10]

When we say that the *Odyssey* contains features of traditional heroic song, we do not, however, give up our right to perform literary criticism on it. Anne Parry and J. B. Hainsworth were surely right to disagree with Lord's assertion that oral poetry cannot be studied by the methods of the literary critic.[11] A *good* literary critic should always have the sense to adapt his methods to the genre in question, of course, but there is no genre which he

---

[9] M. L. West, in the excellent introduction to his text of the *Theogony* (Oxford, 1966).

[10] On these subjects, Lord, *Singer*, and *Serbo-Croatian Heroic Songs* vol. 3 (Cambridge, Mass., 1974), is instructive. On doublets, however, one should certainly consult Bernard Fenik's careful and convincing *Studies in the Odyssey*, *Hermes* Einzelschrift 30 (1974).

[11] Parry, in "Homer as Artist"; see note 3; Hainsworth, in "The Criticism of an Oral Homer", *JHS* 90 (1970), pp. 90-98.

can be commanded to leave to others. For example, the character of Tale of Orošac in *The Wedding of Smailagić Meho* can be analyzed, just as one can analyze Madame Bovary or Huck Finn or Hector, even though we know that Avdo Međedović did not invent Tale or any of his peculiar characteristics. The plot of *Meho* can be analyzed; the values in the work can be discussed. It would be insufferably patronizing *not* to subject *Meho* to the same sort of scrutiny we use on literary works: Avdo was a poet, and *he* chose which traditional plot to present and precisely which traditional language to use in presenting it. The work *as it is presented* is the subject for the literary critic.

In this study, therefore, I shall analyze the *Odyssey* with any methods which seem appropriate to the passage in question. I *do* assume that the work is an essential unity, and I do believe it to have been written. But I do not think that anything I have to say would be substantially different if Apollo himself were to inform the world that Homer couldn't read, or if an apparition straight from the Gate of Horn were to announce publicly that there were six Homers, who took turns composing the *Odyssey*, and that one of them was a monkey with an electric typewriter.

III. THE PENELOPE EPISODE

The extant conclusion of the *Odyssey* can be divided quite neatly into four sections: 1) xxiii, 297-xxiii, 372—this section, which will concern us in the present chapter, will be called the Penelope episode for convenience; 2) xxiv, 1-204, the underworld scene, or Nekuia; 3) xxiv, 205-411, the Laertes section, and 4) xxiv, 412-548, which will be called the Battle episode.

Critics who wish to discredit the Penelope section have not been able to find very much wrong with it archaeologically or linguistically; there are, however, three major lines of argument against the section. The first and most often employed is the argument from authority: Aristarchus, they say, condemned the whole conclusion, from xxiii, 297 to the end of the poem. The second argument relies on guilt by association: lines 344 through 372 clearly prepare the audience for the Laertes and Battle episodes, which the critics have other reasons for wishing to athetize. The third—that inevitable last refuge of desperate scholars—is the aesthetic argument: Odysseus' summary of his adventures is unnecessary, they say, and dull, and therefore bad, and therefore unhomeric.

I shall deal with these points consecutively. At xxiii, 296, codices M, V, and Vindex have the following scholion:

"'Αριστοφάνης δὲ καὶ 'Αρίσταρχος πέρας τῆς 'Οδυσσείας τοῦτο ποιοῦνται."

H, M, Q give us

"τοῦτο τέλος τῆς 'Οδυσσείας φησὶν 'Αρίσταρχος καὶ 'Αριστοφάνης."

And Eustathius tells us:

"'Ιστέον δὲ ὅτι κατὰ τὴν τῶν παλαιῶν ἱστορίαν 'Αρίσταρχος καὶ 'Αριστοράνης, οἱ κορυφαῖοι τῶν τότε γραμματικῶν, εἰς τό, ὡς ἐρρέθη, ἀσπάσιοι λέκτροιο παλαιοῦ θεσμὸν ἵκοντο, περατοῦσι τὴν 'Οδύσσειαν, τὰ ἐφεξῆς ἕως τέλους τοῦ βιβλίου νοθεύοντες."

This seems fairly straightforward, doesn't it? These ancient critics thought the *Odyssey* ended with xxiii, 296. But alas, even on this point we are involved in controversy: the meanings of τέλος and πέρας are disputed. In order to enroll the great Alexandrians on

Our Side, Belzner, Carpenter, Merry, Bethe, Woodhouse and others have maintained that τέλος here means goal, not conclusion.[1] What Aristarchus meant, they say, was that the main action of the plot is finished at this point, although the poem in fact continues for another book. If Aristarchus meant "conclusion" in the usual sense, they argue, then why did he go on to athetize the Nekuia? If he considered the whole thing spurious, wouldn't it have been futile for him to condemn also one particular part of it?

On the question of Aristarchus' special athetesis of the Nekuia, I am not convinced. It is not hard to imagine that he made evaluative distinctions between various interpolations. A cautious scholar, he was perfectly justified in saying, in effect, "X seems to me unhomeric. But Y, which is one part of X, seems even worse than the parts surrounding it. I believe X to be spurious, but I am certain about Y."

The words τέλος and πέρας, however, constitute more of a problem. They *are* ambiguous words. When I first began work on this problem, nearly fifteen years ago, I was persuaded by John Scott's argument for a reading of "end" rather than "goal" for both words —that the Greeks were not monogamous enough to regard *Penelope* as Odysseus' goal.[2] Now, two considerations have caused me to re-examine my position, and to make a proud, unbloodied about-face. First,[3] it still seems likely that *Homer* would not have considered reunion of husband and wife as the goal of his poem, but it is the view of the Alexandrians which is at issue here, not Homer's view, and in the light of Hellenistic values, with their interest in romantic and individualistic plots, it seems possible that Aristarchus and Aristophanes did regard the marital reunion as the climax of the poem. Second, I have now read Hartmut Erbse's discussion of

---

[1] E. Belzner, *Die Komposition der Odysee*, cited favorably by John Scott in his review of the book, *CJ* 8, p. 221, then criticized by Scott in "The Close of the Odyssey", *CJ* 12, p. 397 ff; Rhys Carpenter, *Folk Tale, Fiction and Saga in the Homeric Epics* (Berkeley, 1946), p. 193; W. W. Merry, ed., *Odyssey* (Oxford, 1901), vol. 2, p. 171; E. Bethe, "Der Schluss der Odyssee und Apollonius von Rhodos", *Hermes* 53 (1918), p. 445; Woodhouse, *The Composition of Homer's Odyssey* (Oxford 1930), p. 125.

[2] Scott, "The Close of the Odyssey", p. 397.

[3] For this point, I am grateful to the editors of Mnemosyne. W. B. Stanford, too, observes . . . "I suggest, in that era when uxorious and erotic influences were unusually strong even Aristarchus could have made such a far-reaching error as to end the *Odyssey* at 23, 296." ("The Ending of the Odyssey: an Ethical Approach", *Hermathena* 100 (1965), p. 16.)

the question, and I am particularly impressed by his argument that,
while the Alexandrians had faults as literary critics and as linguists,
it is almost impossible to imagine that they would have allowed
the *Odyssey* to end in mid-sentence, with a μὲν for which there
was no δέ.[4] Therefore, with some slight misgivings, I am now
inclined to the opinion that the Alexandrians did *not* think the
Odyssey ended at xxiii, 296.

It is nice to feel that they are on Our Side after all. But how
important is their support, anyway? The subject of Aristarchus'
trustworthiness has been debated at length, and is generally outside the scope of this study; a few words should suffice. Aristarchus'
opinions are of greater antiquity than, say, Page's, but that fact
should not impress us unduly; in some ways Aristarchus seems to
have been further removed from Homer than we are. Van der Valk
points out,[5] for example, that the Alexandrians frequently athetized
a passage because they considered it obscene or beneath the dignity
of the gods. No critic would do this today, I trust; modern scholars
know more than Aristarchus about early epic and religion, and
realize that frankness about sex and humor about Hera are not
necessarily inconsistent with either literary mastery or simple piety.
We have the advantage over the Alexandrians of possessing a
longer and fuller history and literature from which to draw analogies. We must take the opinions of the ancient critics for what they
are, opinions. I will, accordingly, deal with Aristarchus' objections
to the Nekuia, which are given in detail, but let us dispense with
excessive reverence toward those atheteses of his which are ac-
companied by no evidence.

The second major argument against the Penelope episode is that
it contains two "plants" for later events in the conclusion. By a
"plant" I mean an anticipatory reference, which is not stressed
excessively at the time it occurs, but which prepares the listener or
reader to accept the later event as natural, logical, or expected.
Both the *Iliad* and the *Odyssey* contain many plants—in fact, subtle
"planting" is a striking characteristic of the Homeric style, which
contributes greatly to the feelings of unity, realism, and inexorability
which most readers carry away from either epic. Planting is, incidentally, a characteristic which I would be more inclined to

---

[4] H. Erbse, *Beiträge*, p. 171.

[5] M.H.A.L.H. Van der Valk, *Textual Criticism of the Odyssey*, (Leiden,
1949).

associate with written than with oral poetry.[6] For example, *The Wedding of Smailagić Meho*, while not by any means a contemptible poem, would have been greatly improved if Avdo had better anticipated the turns he was going to let his plot take. There is a scene in which the hero and heroine return to the heroine's home *just* at the moment the heroine's mother is about to commit suicide by defenestration. They rescue her, of course. It is a ludicrous scene. It is "unreal." Homer would not have allowed such a scene; he would have prepared for it, perhaps by having his heroine remark, at some point on the journey, something like "I'm really worried about Mother. She's been so depressed lately; I'm afraid she might do something terrible. Let's hurry!" At some other point, he might casually slip in a reference to the extreme height of the palace in which Fatima's mother lives. The audience would scarcely notice these references at the time, but when the melodramatic moment arrived, the suicide scene would strike them as somehow "real" and appropriate. Perhaps "planting" is not pathognomonic of literacy; perhaps it is merely characteristic of narrative skill, whether literary or oral. At any rate, it is characteristic of Homer, and there are two important plants in the Penelope episode.

First (359-60) "And now I am going to the wooded farm to see my excellent father. . ." Second, following right after the first, Odysseus tells Penelope to keep to her room, since he fears retribution from the suitors' kinsmen. The hero and Telemachus and Eumaeus and Philoitius arm themselves and leave the palace under protection of Athene. These lines so clearly prepare for episodes 3 and 4 of the conclusion that if they are kept, the later material (excluding the Nekuia) must be, too. Now, let us assume for the sake of argument that Book xxiv is wholly spurious. We therefore automatically reject xxiii, 344 to end (the aforementioned plants); now, where are we to conclude our *Odyssey*? There are in Book xxiii only four good stopping points, 296, 299, 309, and 343. All others would leave us in the middle of something. (Of course the original *Odyssey may* have ended in the middle of something, but it would seem perverse to assume so, to reject an artistically complete poem which we have in hand in favor of a conjectured incomplete one.) Let us examine the four possible stopping places.

---

[6] For a further discussion of planting, see "Homer, Avdo Mededović, and *The Elephant's Child*", pp. 330-1.

xxiii, 296: Has the advantage of being an impressive last line, has, perhaps, the authority of Aristarchus, would omit the epitome, which has been so often vilified.

Objections: An ending at this point would leave an uncompleted μὲν in the last line. Second (an argument of Scott as well as Armstrong),[7] it is un-Homeric (and in fact, un-Greek) to end a literary work on a private rather than a public note. Homer likes to move in a crowd; a closeup of a hero alone is generally followed by the hero's rejoining the army, the sailors, or the court. Society ratifies the success of the individual and confirms his failures; the audience is presumably not satisfied with learning the outcome of one man's actions until it knows also how everybody else reacted (and often how the gods reacted, too.) "It is contrary to all reason and sentiment," says Armstrong,[8] "That either the Iliad or the Odyssey should close with a 'so they went to bed' finale."

299: supplies a compliment for μὲν: "αὐτὰρ Τηλέμαχος. . ." Also omits the summary. Mentions Telemachus, the herds, and the women, and is thus less private than an ending at 296 would be, but still surely not enough to satisfy Armstrong's and Scott's requirement for a crowd scene with final bows. (F. L. Kay [9] would end the poem at this point. In addition to the μὲν problem, he calls attention to the awkwardness of τὼ in 300, which refers back 4 lines. If the "continuer" had begun his task at line 297, argues Kay, he would not have put himself in the position of having to use such an awkward dual. But if lines 297-299 existed already, he would find this necessary, to make the subject of line 300 clear. This argument seems a trifle weak: if the τὼ is really so awkward, couldn't the "continuer" have referred to Odysseus and Penelope by name? Weak or not, however, it seems clear that this argument of Kay's does not really support an ending at 296, and thus could be listed under any of our alternative stopping-places.)

309: Still omits the detailed summary, and is a rather nice line to conclude with, but still would end the poem on a personal note.

343: is another lovely line, but this would still furnish a private ending, and it includes the full epitome.

These later three, then, would avoid the unfulfilled μὲν difficulty,

---

[7] James I. Armstrong, "The Marriage Song—Od 23", *TAPA* 89 (1958), pp. 38-43. Scott, "The Close of the Odyssey", p. 404.

[8] Armstrong, *op. cit.*, p. 39.

[9] F. L. Kay, "Aristarchus' 'τέλος', *Odyssey* xxiii, 296", *CR* (1957), p. 106.

but have the disadvantage of having no really positive arguments in their favor, not even the authority of the Alexandrians. All three are 'private'—all are nice lines—there is not much to choose among them, except that the last includes the summary.

In sum, if we are convinced by Armstrong's arguments, none of these four possible endings is satisfactory, and we will have to proceed to the end of Book xxiv (with or without omission of the Nekuia) before we will find another stopping-place. If we admit the μὲν problem, but reject the argument about public versus private endings, then we still do not know which of three lines is the 'real' end of the *Odyssey*, and we shall never be able to decide on one, for in this choice we will not have even the frail reed of Alexandrian dogmatism to lean on. The reader's final decision will, I suppose, depend on which way he is personally disposed to frame the Homeric question, whether "How much Homer can I legitimately leave standing?", or, "How much Homer can I possibly cut out?"

To the reader who asks the former question, this chapter has thus far indicated, I trust, that there are no compelling reasons for his rejecting any of Book xxiii, unless our later examination of the Laertes and Battle episodes should force us to excise 344 through 372. As for the critic who asks the latter question, I hope he has gathered from the preceding discussion that he might run into some difficulties with an ending in xxiii. However, since he is a man who asks *"Must* I leave this in?" rather than *"May* I?", he will probably have decided for the earliest possible stopping-place, 299 or 309, as either would omit the summary of Odysseus' adventures.

Let us now proceed to the abhorred summary, and ask, is it really so offensive?—and, more important, is it uncharacteristic of Homer? In other words, *may* we leave it in?

First, how bad is it, as summaries go? It is not very long (only 31 lines to summarize eight books); the adventures are told simply, in chronological order, unlike the original account. In fact, Mme. Dacier [10] considered this chronological clarification to be the *raison d'être* of the epitome. It is long for a passage in indirect discourse, but what else could Homer use?—the actual narration took the whole night. (Cauer [11] considers the very use of indirect

---

[10] F. A. G. Spohn, *Commentatio de Extrema Odysseae Parte* (Leipzig, 1816), quotes Mme Dacier, *L'Odyssée d'Homère*, 1.1.

[11] Paul Cauer, *Grundfragen der Homerkritik* (Leipzig, 1923), pp. 430-1.

discourse in this passage a sign of lateness, but he gives no clear evidence for his position: indeed, his discussion of the passage is concerned almost exclusively with how cleverly the 'continuator' has handled the scene.) And is the epitome appropriate to the context at this point in the poem? Certainly—Penelope would surely expect some explanation for her husband's long absence, and this is not only a full account but a tactful one: Circe, although our hero spent a full year enjoying her company, is brushed off in one disparaging line: "καὶ Κίρκης κατέλεξε δόλον πολυμηχανίην τε," while of Calypso he says that in spite of her offers—"οὔ ποτε θυμὸν ἐνὶ στήθεσσιν ἔπειθεν." This is not quite the impression we got from Book v, where the phrase is "οὐκέτι ἥνδανε νύμφη"—the maid *no longer* gave him pleasure, although he continued to sleep with her. The memorable Nausicaa is omitted altogether. There is also rather a subjective, boastful tone to the whole account (only *I* escaped— nobody ever got by Scylla before *me*—Calypso loved me; see what I gave up for you, dear?—the Phaeacians treated me like a god—) which would seem amusingly characteristic both of Odysseus specifically and generally of any man retelling experiences to his admiring wife, in the privacy of their bedroom.

But is the summary necessary? Allen thinks not:[12] "Such an epitome is obviously useless to the reader of the Odyssey .... I was wrong, however, to say [in an earlier work] that Homer never epitomizes nor recapitulates his action." The two parts of this statement are intimately connected, and I will deal with them together. That is, the summary *could* be cut out without real damage to the structure of the *Odyssey*; on the other hand, just such super-fluousness seems to be an inescapable characteristic of the Homeric poems. The *Iliad* and the *Odyssey* are filled with passages—descriptions, repeated speeches and similes, summaries of familiar material and so forth—which are not strictly necessary. To the average modern reader, who admires freshness and 'tight' structure, these passages are merely uninteresting; they represent waste matter to be cleared away. He will forgive repeated epithets and verbal formulae; he can appreciate their usefulness to the oral poet, and perhaps can dimly sense their positive value as evocative word-magic, but whole passages are too much for him. He has forgotten

---

[12] T. W. Allen, *Homer, the Origins and the Transmission* (Oxford, 1924), p. 220.

what it is like to listen rather than to read. Listeners forget things; they fail to hear things. It takes a longer time to listen than to read: by the time a bard had reached Book xxiii in his recital of the *Odyssey*, the adventure with Calypso was a thing of the past, having taken place days before.

Homer often helps his listeners along; for example, with the often criticized second council of gods. The first council had already taken notice of Odysseus' plight, and the gods had decided to send Hermes to the rescue. After four books of Ithaca and Telemachus, however, the audience might be expected to have forgotten Odysseus' pitiable position—they could not forget Odysseus himself nor his greatness, for Homer assiduously inserts reminders of the hero wherever possible, but they might well be hazy as to precisely where he was now and whether anything was being done about it. So the poet helpfully adds the second Olympian council, to get across the vital information about Calypso and Hermes.

Odysseus' epitome to Penelope in xxiii is a helpful clarification of a similar sort; it straightens out the chronology of the sea-adventures and sets them out succinctly, so the audience may admire the whole intricate pattern which it has already seen in fragments. Homer was no doubt proud of his story and wanted to make sure his hearers remembered what they had heard. If we accept the whole 'continuation,' we will find all three major plots of the *Odyssey* summarized in the course of the poem, the Telemachy in Book xvii, the Sea-Tales here, and the Revenge in Book xxiv.

Is there any analogy for this in the *Iliad*? There is. In Book I, Achilles gives his mother a detailed, formal summary of his quarrel with Agamemnon; in xviii, Thetis tells Hephaistos the basic plot of the *Iliad* up to that point. These are useful clarifying scenes: the first makes sure that the audience knows how it all started, while the second, like Odysseus' epitome, succinctly reviews the story, so that the hearer can see and admire the beautiful whole design, no longer as a scroll unwinding scene by scene, but as an intricate mural viewed at a glance. The major difference between these *Iliad* epitomes and those of the *Odyssey* is in their appropriateness to dramatic context: the first *Iliad* summary is, as Achilles himself points out with charming naiveté, contextually unnecessary since Thetis as a divinity knows the whole story of the quarrel already. The second, to Hephaistos, would seem to be unnecessary for the same reason, and certainly includes more detail than is required for persuading the blacksmith to make the armor. All three *Odyssey* epitomes, however, are told to hearers who do not and cannot know the stories involved, and who have strong personal reasons for wishing to hear them.

For the preceding reasons, then, I believe that the Book xxiii epitome is not only characteristic of the Homeric manner, but also a useful and effective device, particularly in a work composed for oral performance. I can therefore see no compelling reason for rejecting any of Book xxiii; accordingly, let us prepare to descend into a murkier region.

IV. IN HADES' HALLS

Cyllenian Hermes leads the souls of the suitors to the land of the dead; there, in the meadow of asphodel, they encounter Achilles, Patroclus, Antilochus, Ajax, and Agamemnon. Achilles comments on Agamemnon's unhappy doom; Agamemnon answers with a benediction on Achilles: "ὄλβιε Πηλέος υἱέ, θεοῖς ἐπιείκελ' Ἀχιλλεῦ" ". . . you are a fortunate man," he says, (in contrast to me), because you died at Troy and had a splendid funeral. After describing that funeral at some length, Agamemnon catches sight of the suitors and questions one of them, Amphimedon, who replies with a summary of the domestic plot of the *Odyssey*. Although Agamemnon is a family friend of Amphimedon's, and that luckless shade has just concluded his speech with a pitiful description of his own present condition, bloody, unburied and unwept, Agamemnon's only thought is of Odysseus: "ὄλβιε Λαέρταο πάϊ, πολυμήχαν' Ὀδυσσεῦ—," he says, and concludes his apostrophe with a blessing on Penelope and a curse on his own evil wife.

And that is what went on ὑπὸ κεύθεσι γαίης. These proceedings received special condemnation from Aristarchus, and have not fared much better in the succeeding centuries. Even many of the staunchest Unitarians have been willing to concede this battle, and have contented themselves with trying to salvage the rest of xxiv from the critical holocaust.

What is it about this scene that has evoked so much scorn? Objections to the Nekuia can be divided into five categories. First, the minor Aristarchan criticisms: 'Cyllenian' Hermes is, for Homer, a *hapax legomenon*; there is no 'Rock Leukas' on the way to Hades' house; to number the nine Muses is not Homeric. Second, a rather more important Artistarchan objection: Hermes as *psychopompus* is not Homeric; why could not the suitors go to the underworld unassisted, as in the *Iliad*? Third, another Aristarchan objection: the suitors are unburied. How can they mingle with the other shades? Fourth, Amphimedon's summary is incorrect: he says that Odysseus came home just as Penelope had finally finished and washed the shroud for Laertes, whereas the shroud had actually been finished for some time at the beginning of the *Odyssey*; also, he says that Penelope and Odysseus together planned the

bow-stringing trick, but actually Penelope was not in on the secret.
The last objection to the Nekuia, as might be expected, is aesthetic:
the episode is unnecessary and holds up the progress of the plot;
the conversation between Achilles and Agamemnon, especially,
is, in Page's words, an "enormous irrelevance";[1] the whole scene
is filled with repetitions, and it ends abruptly.

We will discuss these five groups of objections in order, taking
up the first three in the present chapter and the latter two in
Chapter Five. First let us dispose of Cyllenian Hermes, the Rock
Leukas, and the nine Muses. Cyllenian Hermes is mentioned only
this once by Homer, but, as Shewan points out,[2] Smintheus Apollo
is also a *hapax legomenon*. The Rock Leukas, the Gates of the Sun,
and the City of Dreams were not mentioned on Odysseus' voyage,
but then, as Lang suggests,[3] he was a mortal travelling by ship
from some vague point in fairyland, while the suitors are dead
men travelling from Ithaca by what may have been a perfectly
ordinary route for souls. Shewan has suggested that *Leukas Petre*
is the prominent cape at the end of the island of Leukas, a sort of
Land's End for sailors travelling West, and thus a likely first land-
mark on a voyage from the known world to the unknown.[4] As for
the nine Muses, Lang says,[5] "It is urged that the Muses were not
known as Nine till the arts had been differentiated and classified.
But the ninefold division may be due to the number of the Muses."

All these are, I suppose, reasonable explanations, and will perhaps satisfy those who are deeply disturbed by uncertainties about
the geography of Hell, the same troubled souls who expend a good
deal of thought on questions like 'how old was Nestor by the time
Telemachus met him?', 'would Odysseus' raft have been seaworthy?'
and 'how could the Achaeans have built that wall so fast?' College
students are particularly prone to such worries; as they grow
older, most of them simply stop reading Homer—a few start making
maps of the voyages of Odysseus, showing where he *really* went.
However, for those of us who do not mind fiction, and can tolerate
a moderate amount of uncertainty, no explanations for "Cyllenian"
or "Rock Leukas" seem pressingly necessary. To the question, "why

---

[1] Page, *Homeric Odyssey, op. cit.*, p. 119.
[2] A. Shewan, "The Continuation of the Odyssey", *CP* 9 (1914).
[3] Andrew Lang, *Homer and the Epic* (London, 1893), p. 316-17.
[4] A. Shewan, p. 173.
[5] Lang, *op. cit.*, p. 317.

did Homer say Cyllenian Hermes, Rock Leukas, Nine Muses, and so on?', it seems to us that a perfectly good answer is 'why not?' Someone—whether Homer or a rhapsode or a forger—used these novel expressions, or they would not be in our text. Why should it have been someone else and not Homer?

Now, what about Hermes Psychopompus? Lang would put him in the category we have just discussed:[6] "We do not know, of course, whether the function of Hermes is a novelty; Homer has had no previous occasion to describe it . . ." But this is not, I feel, quite so trivial a matter as the Rock Leukas. After all, the Nekuia does not stand or fall by any one of the phrases in our first category; the Rock Leukas, or the Nine, or "Cyllenian" could any one of them be cut out without serious damage to the episode, but the presence of Hermes is fundamental. Homer has described death before, many times, but as Denys Page puts it in his delightfully pre-judiced prose,[7] "This function of Hermes, probably a very old one, is elsewhere absolutely suppressed by the Homeric poets."

This statement calls for examination. First of all, as to the antiquity of Hermes' connection with *psychopompia*, there seems to be little disagreement among modern authorities. Under 'Hermes' in Pauly-Wissowa,[8] Stein says that Hermes' function in xxiv is "augenscheinlich keine freie Erfindung des späten Dichters, son-dern eine Entlehnung aus einem verbreiteten Volksglauben." Rohde,[9] although stressing that it is an innovation for Homer, considers it likely that Hermes' *psychopompia* is "borrowed from the ancient folk-belief of some remote corner of Greece." Otto agrees:[10] "The notion is . . . abundantly documented in cults and myths." Farnell suggests that "the conception of Hermes as the guardian of souls goes back at least to the oldest period of the Homeric poems." [11] H. L. Lorimer, too, says, "the function of Hermes in Ω is not necessarily a mark of lateness. . . . Hermes in this episode is not a messenger but an escort and, more than that,

---

[6] *Ibid.*, p. 316.

[7] Page, *op. cit.*, p. 117.

[8] Stein, "Hermes," *RE* (1913).

[9] Erwin Rohde, *Psyche* (New York, 1925), pp. 8-9.

[10] Walter P. Otto, *The Homeric Gods*, trans by Moses Hadas (New York, 1957), p. 113.

[11] L. R. Farnell, *Greek Hero Cults and Ideas of Immortality* (Oxford, 1921), p. 10.

an escort of the dead. It is his chthonic character that makes him
peculiarly suited to this mission here." [12] Like Page, all five of these
authorities apparently consider the Nekuia spurious and 'late,' but
all are nevertheless agreed that the author of xxiv did not invent
this function of the god. It existed in Homer's time or earlier, in
the Mind of the Folk, or at least in the minds of some of the folks.
Why, then, did Homer elsewhere neglect (or to use Page's term
absolutely suppress) this picturesque piece of lore? Did Homer
reject a belief in Hermes as an escort of souls, and did he cling to
the opinion that they always traveled αὐτόμαται to the underworld,
ὡς ἐν 'Ιλιάδι (to use Aristarchus' phrase)? Was he suppressing a
popular superstition and promoting a more enlightened (or more
attractive, or more pious) conception of the afterlife, and was it
only a late *Bearbeiter* who allowed this *Volksglaube* to contaminate
Homer's otherwise pure and consistent theology?

How pure and consistent *are* Homer's conceptions of death and
the afterlife? Let us look at the *Iliad*, which deals with Death and
deaths more than does the *Odyssey*. First of all, there are the purely
physical deaths: the soul, or 'life,' leaves the bones, the limbs or
the nostrils, or escapes by a wound; or darkness or a mist covers
the eyes; the limbs' strength is broken; life and strength are 'scat-
tered'—here there seems to be some conflict as to where, precisely,
the soul resides in a living man. When it escapes by a wound, it
seems to reside in the blood; at other times it seems to be the same
thing as 'strength' (in the bones or limbs); at still others, it seems
to be equated with sight or consciousness (see especially V, 696
to 698 and XXII, 467, where the 'life' leaves someone who has
merely fainted); at still others 'Life' seems to mean 'breath.'
(Lest we be too hard on Homer the physiologist, let us remember
that even 20th century scientists and physicians have a hard time
trying to define precisely wherein life resides and what precisely
constitutes death.) Continuing with the physical descriptions, we
also find Castor and Pollux held by the 'life-giving earth.' It may
be objected that none of these examples has any bearing on the
case, since it is not death but the afterlife which concerns us;
nevertheless, they are useful, I think, in showing that even in a
concrete physical area Homer's idea of death was a hazy one:
he was not sure exactly what a soul *was*.

---

[12] H. L. Lorimer, *Homer and the Monuments* (London, 1950), p. 484.

And when we come to the life beyond, we find the mist gathering even darker. Souls do travel, generally *down*, to the House of Hades, just as Aristarchus told us. But they are also *hurled*; often they *flutter*, and twice, they seem to *walk*, along a definite road.

These latter examples are interesting; in Book XIII, 414-16, Deiphobus, having killed Hypsenor, the slayer of his friend Asios, boasts that now Asios will be cheerful as he goes down to Hades, since he will have an escort. In Book XIV, 454-57, Poulydamas makes a similar taunt; his javelin will be a stick for Prothoenor to lean on as he makes his journey to Death's house. Harry L. Levy [13] has suggested that these jocular boasts, like some aspects of Patroclus' funeral, represent an "unconscious survival of an earlier eschatology." No doubt these references to a really physical journey after death *do* stem ultimately from a more primitive era of belief than Homer's, but how unconscious can we expect our poet to be? Are we to believe that Homer did not understand what he was saying when he repeated these grim army jokes? Could there be any point to these brutal jests if there remained no lingering feeling (in Homer's audience, if not in Homer) that the afterlife might actually be like that?

Patroclus' funeral should clear up any doubts: Achilles asks the Achaeans (XXIII, 50-1) to pile up wood and beside it, "whatever is fitting for the dead man to have as he goes under the murky darkness."

And they do so: his pyre is piled with sheep, cattle, oil, honey, horses, dogs, and twelve Trojan captives. Achilles did not dedicate them in memory of Patroclus, or present them as a sacrifice to a god, or burn them as a public display of his grief and his friend's worth; he merely gave his friend 'What is fitting for a dead man to have on his journey.' And yet here, too, there is inconsistency; in his dream appearance to Achilles, Patroclus indicates clearly that even before the funeral he has once already made the journey to Hades' gates. We will return to this speech later—suffice it to say that Achilles' gifts to the pyre are, in keeping with the hero's usual character, excessive—Patroclus does not apparently need them. All he asks for is to be burned swiftly and to share an urn with Achilles. The Achaeans, however, make no comment or protest

---

[13] Harry P. Levy, "Echoes of Early Eschatology in the *Iliad*," *AJP* (1948), pp. 420-1.

about the lavish funeral; no-one acts as though Achilles' arrange-
ments were in any way peculiar or incomprehensible; no-one says
"he won't need those things where he's going," because, presumably, they thought their departed comrade *might* just possibly
need them.

So much for the souls that travel "αὐτόμαται." *Some* souls are
carried away, by the Keres or by Death. With some the image is
more active; Idaios escapes the black Ker in the nick of time
(V, 22); Death runs faster than Sokos and catches him (XI, 451);
Death, 'the spiritbreaker,' is poured around Aphareus (XIII, 544);
Zeus wards off the Keres from Sarpedon (XII, 402), but Death
eventually closes the eyes and nostrils of the young man (XVI, 502).
In some instances Death or the Keres are personified quite vividly:
the Keres drive the sons of Merops on to their destruction (XI, 332),
the Keres brought the Achaeans to Troy in their black ships (viii,
528); Sarpedon sees Keres by the myriads standing around him
and Glaucus (XII, 326); Zeus says that Death stands close beside
Hector as he dons Achilles' armor (XVII, 202); Deukalion (XX, 481)
looks Death in the face; Death is the brother of Sleep (XIV, 231),
and finally, Sleep and Death carry Sarpedon's body to Lycia. It is
difficult to determine, in most of these passages, just how figurative
Death and the Keres are. Often they seem to be mere figures of
speech, as when Deukalion looks death in the face; sometimes,
however, they are real beings, real divinities who take an active
part in the lives of men. A figure of speech could not, after all,
carry Sarpedon's real corpse to the real country of Lycia.

How well do these concepts fit in with the scheme in which a
man's 'life,' expelled from a wound in his body by human agency,
or released somehow from his bones, flutters or walks to the house
of Hades of the gates, or of the horses? The answer is, not at all.
In fact, conflicting views of death can perhaps be found uneasily
united in the same sentence, (XV, 251-2). Speaking of a near escape,
Hector says, "Indeed on that day it seemed that I would go to
the corpses and the house of Hades (νέκυας καὶ δῶμ' 'Αΐδαο), when
I had breathed out my dear life." It will perhaps be objected that
νέκυας here are simply 'the dead,' the shades in the underworld;
nonetheless, the juxtaposition of νέκυας, δῶμ' 'Αΐδαο and φίλον
ἄιον ἦτορ would seem unusually cavalier if Homer knew what he
believed about death and the afterlife, and wanted to present those
beliefs consistently.

To complete the picture of confusion, we need only refer to XX,
61-65. "Aidoneus, ruler of the dead below, was afraid; he jumped
from his throne and shouted, fearing that Poseidon the Earth-
shaker might break open the earth above him, and men and gods
might see his household, terrible and decaying (εὐρώεντα), which
even the gods abhor." Now, what would be so abhorrent and
terrible about the appearance of a hall full of dreamlike, disembodied shades? A depressing sight, no doubt, but hardly enough
to justify σμερδαλέ᾽ εὐρώεντα (Lattimore's phrase is "ghastly and
mouldering"),[14] unless οἱ ἔνεροι of line 61 are half seen as *corpses*,
and Aidoneus' kingdom as the earth's graveyards (which seem
more likely to be opened up by an earthquake than do the halls of
Hades.) Gods and men might indeed shudder at *that* sight. Is not
this the same grisly breaking-open of graves envisioned by the
prophet Isaiah, when he said, "the foundations of the earth do
shake (xxiv, 18) . . . the earth shall cast out the dead . . . For, be-
hold, the Lord cometh out of his place to punish the inhabitants
of the earth for their iniquity: the earth also shall disclose her
blood, and shall no more cover her slain"? (xxiv, 19, 21.) The chief
difference is that Isaiah is deadly serious; he conceives of the
impending catastrophe as a moral event, a judgment, while Homer
presents his earthquake in the semi-humorous context of the
Theomachia. Comic hyperbole is characteristic of those Homeric
scenes in which the gods play at being men, and this fanciful vision,
in which the august Aidoneus jumps, screams, and trembles, is
quite in keeping, albeit in a grim way, with the rest of the episode.
The point which should interest us, however, is that here, as always
in the *Iliad*, Homer uses that picture of death and the afterlife
which suits him best. His "beliefs" shift and vary according to
the requirements of his literary context. Sometimes he views death
literally, as a familiar physical process; sometimes he views it
with solemn awe, as a mysterious journey to a murky realm;
sometimes that journey loses mystery and gains primitive concrete-
ness, as it becomes a road along which the dead walk, leaning on
staffs, escorted by slaves bearing meat, honey, oil, and wine; sometimes death is a mere figure of speech, bringing the Achaeans to
Troy or standing near men in danger; sometimes He becomes a full-

---

[14] Richmond Lattimore, trans., *The Iliad of Homer* (Chicago, 1951),
p. 406.

fledged deity, capable of carrying the fully physical corpse of Sarpedon from Troy to Lycia, a deity whose brother Sleep carries on a long conversation with Hera in Book XIV.

In pointing out that VIII, 16 and 480 present contradictory evidence for the geographical position of Tartarus, C. M. Bowra said,[15] "In this cosmogony Homer incorporates many different views of the world, just as he has different views of the life after death. He was not concerned with exactitude in such matters." Homer's gods are similarly literary and similarly inconsistent, as has been noticed by Alfred Schlesinger, George Calhoun and others.[16] In a brightly written discussion, Schlesinger has suggested that Homer himself probably believed the gods to be omnipresent and omniscient, but that it was often more convenient or more vivid for him to present them as limited in a human way. For example, when they wanted to, the gods could apparently travel anywhere 'as fast as thought,' but at other times they required horses and carriages, and gates had to be opened for them to pass through. "We must distinguish," says Schlesinger, "between theology and creative imagination. In recent times few, I suppose, have mistaken Homer for a theologian." [17] His thought is echoed by B. C. Dietrich; "It is impossible to succeed in an attempt at establishing a uniform Homeric theology." [18]

The *Iliad* and the *Odyssey* are works of fiction, not sermons or essays. Like Virgil, like Milton, Homer apparently possessed numerous, varied, mutually contradictory theological traditions to draw on—and drew on any or all of them as needed. The poet of the *Odyssey* (whether or not he was also the poet of the *Iliad*) may have had even more sources to draw from (Egyptian or 'Eastern') than did the composer of the presumably earlier work. "No one," says John Scott, "could reconstruct Milton's theology from his poetry, if that poetry were the only source of our knowledge;" [19]

---

[15] Bowra, *op. cit.*, p. 264

[16] George M. Calhoun, "Homer's Gods: Prolegomena," *Trans. Phil. As.* 68, (1937), pp. 11-25; Calhoun, "Homer's Gods—Myth and Marchen," *AJP* (1939), pp. 1-28; Calhoun, "The Divine Entourage in Homer," *AJP* 61 (1940), pp. 257-77; Alfred G. Schlesinger, "The Literary Necessity of Anthropomorphism," *CJ* 32 (1936), pp. 19-26.

[17] Schlesinger, *op. cit.*, p. 19.

[18] B. C. Dietrich, *Death, Fate and the Gods* (London, Athlone Press 1967), pp. 188-9.

[19] Scott, *The Unity of Homer* (Berkeley, 1921), p. 134.

the same is true of Virgil and, I believe, of Homer. In fact, this state of affairs is less surprising in Homer than in Milton, for the theology of the Greeks was traditionally over-inclusive rather than dogmatic. From a literary point of view there is a distinct advantage in a loose polytheistic system which lacks both a powerful priesthood and a Bible; it enables poets to welcome and use any piece of new or 'foreign' lore which seems attractive.

In addition, the life beyond death has always been a fertile field for speculation, since so few of us have been as privileged as Heracles or Dante or Aeneas. As Farnell says (speaking of Patroclus' funeral,) [20] "We may indeed say that those offerings are inconsistent with the usual Homeric conception of the disembodied soul as a feeble wraith; but who is always consistent in this dim region of thought?" In 20th century America, believing Christians can be heard to say "It's as hot as the hinges of Hades," and avowed atheists may refer to death as "marching up to the pearly gates." Each of us probably has his private feelings about the life beyond; some of us, no doubt, have worked our convictions out into self-consistent systems, but publicly we westerners have as common property a large collection of different myths about death; St. Peter guards the gates of heaven in our jokes, but Charon still ferries the dead in our poetry.

Bearing all this in mind, can we deny Homer his Hermes Psychopompus, used only once but used effectively? He does not say that Hermes leads all souls to the underworld, only that he led these souls; the god is introduced here for literary, not theological, reasons. And what are they? I can think of three reasons why the souls should be led by a god, and three reasons why that god should be Hermes.

Why the souls are led by a god: First the introduction of a deity is the easiest and most effective way to give importance and dignity to any piece of action. Homer is concluding his story; the climax is over, and his audience is perhaps tired, but he has several things still to say for which he wants his hearers' attention. One trip to the underworld has already taken place, and the business he wants to accomplish in this scene is basically human and natural, not mysterious and dramatic as in Book xi. He therefore tries to avoid the anticlimax by a solemn, elaborate introduction. Whether

---

[20] Farnell, *op. cit.*, p. 6.

or not he succeeds is an aesthetic question. The general consensus seems to be that he does not (. . .even Van der Valk, who thinks the Nekuia undoubtedly genuine, calls the episode "overcharged.")[21] I disagree, but of course this is not the appropriate place for aesthetic judgments.

Second, and corollary to the first statement, deaths of important characters in the *Iliad* are generally treated differently from and more elaborately than the ordinary deaths of nonentities. As we have seen, most men simply die, meet fate, fly off to the house of Hades, are covered by darkness and so forth, but Sarpedon, Patroclus, and Hector receive special treatment. In Sarpedon's case there is Zeus' indecision and bloody tears and the spiriting away of his body; he is also the first character in the poem to make a deathbed speech. Patroclus is struck by Apollo, then by Euphorbus, and finally by Hector; he, too, makes a dying speech, exhibiting prophetic powers; his final release is marked by the pathetic image of the fluttering soul mourning her destiny as she leaves youth and manhood behind her, and he returns to earth as a ghost. Hector's death is marked by the balancing of the golden scales, by the agency of Athene, by another prophetic speech, by the repetition of the image of the mourning soul, and by the miraculous preservation of his body. In similar fashion, the death of the suitors, the only important death in the Odyssey, is fittingly marked by unusual circumstances and by divine assistance.

Third, as Samuel Bassett suggests,[22] a guide is dramatically necessary to initiate the action of the Nekuia, to get the souls of the suitors moving. Since their death, in Book xxii, the shades presumably have been resting passively, waiting for Homer to find time to dispose of them; they must now make their appearance on stage, and the introduction of a guide makes their sudden entrance smoother from a dramatic standpoint.

In Book xxii, twenty-one suitors are killed; twenty-one separate deaths are described. Not *one* is characterized by the formula "his soul went down to Hades' house," or by any words which describe what happened to the suitor's shade after death. This might, of course, be coincidence. But it also might be quite deliberate: it certainly *looks* as if the author of the Slaughter of the Suitors

---

[21] Van der Valk, *op. cit.*, p. 240.

[22] Samuel Eliot Bassett, "The Second Necyia Again", *AJP* (1923), pp. 43-53.

(who surely has as much right as anyone to the name Homer) was already planning the Nekuia, and wanted to keep all twenty-one souls in reserve for their journey together in Book xxiv. To my mind, this is important (if 'silent') evidence for the genuineness of the Nekuia.

Now, why should Hermes be the god chosen to escort the suitors?

First, he performs a similar function at the end of the *Iliad*. First he is urged by the gods to steal the body of Hector; then he escorts Priam at night on his journey to recover the body. This mission has chthonic overtones, and he is an escort; it is not, of course, *psychopompia*, but it suggests it, and more important is the simple fact that—although generally unimportant in the *Iliad*— he plays an important part in the last book of that epic. If the *Odyssey* is in some ways a deliberate sequel to the *Iliad*, as I believe it is, Hermes' appearance in the Nekuia may be an echo of the conclusion of the earlier epic.

Second, that Hermes had underworld connections in Homer's period is suggested by vii, 136-8, a passage in which the Phaeacians are described as pouring libations to the Giant-slayer before retiring to bed. Farnell [23] (who mistakenly cites the ninth book) says, "The Greeks of the later period had the same custom. Was it not done to secure the god's protection from the terror of ghostly visitations?" Other chthonic connections are suggested by xi 626, which tells of his escorting Heracles to the underworld, and xxiv, 343 and 445, which refer to him as lord of sleep.[24]

Hermes has a special function in the *Odyssey*, and this is his final bow. It is appropriate that both he and Athene should appear in the concluding episodes of the poem, for the two of them (and not Athene alone) are Odysseus' guardian deities.

Athene's conspicuous absence from the sea-wandering adventures has occasioned some critical comment, for her explanation to the hero (that she did not want to offend Uncle Poseidon) is manifestly lame. Poseidon's grievance stemmed from the Polyphemus episode; why, then did Athene not help Odysseus before (and during) that

---

[23] Farnell, *op. cit.*, p. 10.

[24] Agathe Thornton, in *People & Themes in Homer's Odyssey* (Dunedin, N.Z., 1970), pp. 4-5, has also noticed that the suitors' souls were left, waiting, in the slaughter episode; she also points out that Hermes and Athene are a team in Book i, and that at the end of xxiii, Athene's leading Odysseus and his supporters out of town in daylight is "parallel and contrasted" with the *psychopompia* of Hermes here.

unfortunate adventure? Surely Poseidon's anger is an excuse of
Homer's, put in to hide the poet's real, literary reasons for banishing
the goddess. What, then, were the poet's real reasons? Woodhouse [25]
suggests that in the pre-Homeric tradition, Athene was absent
because it was her wrath which vexed the nostoi of all the heroes;
Homer kept the tradition of her non-intervention but changed her
motivation. Besides, says Woodhouse, Homer did not want Odysseus
to seem like an automaton; therefore, the tradition of Athene's
absence from the sea-tales suited his literary needs. Woodhouse
presents good evidence for Athene's original wrath: iii, 132-6—
"Then Zeus devised a woeful homecoming for the Argives...
many of them found disaster through the destructive wrath of the
grey-eyed daughter of the Great Father," and iii, 143-6, "He
(Agamemnon) wanted to detain the host and to sacrifice holy
hecatombs to appease Athene's terrible anger—fool, he did not
know she would remain unmoved," as well as iv, 502, "Then he
(Aias the lesser) would have escaped his fate—in spite of Athene's
enmity—if he had not be boastful—," and so we may perhaps agree
with one-half of Woodhouse's argument, that in leaving Athene
out of Odysseus' wanderings, Homer was following an older tradition in which the goddess actually caused those wanderings.

But why did he choose to follow that tradition as far as he did?
After all, he had already departed from it in not making her wrath
responsible for Odysseus' misfortunes—this, clearly, because he
wanted to retain Athene as his hero's good guardian—certainly
Homer could have departed one step further, actually bringing her
into the sea-tales, if he had wanted to? The automaton hypothesis
really seems insufficient: Odysseus is no automaton in the Ithacan
adventure; although Athene appears frequently, she limits her aid
to advice and encouragement, often doing no more than giving
divine ratification to his hero's own ideas. A solution to this problem
is suggested by Anne Amory Parry:[26] "Athena, as the goddess of
wisdom, stands for Odysseus' *total* σοφία, and it is appropriate that
she does not appear while he is in the process of acquiring the
various separate parts of his knowledge." Amory sees the sea-tales
as a *Bildungsroman*; Odysseus starts out clever and emerges Wise,
and Athene is the divine representative of his wisdom.

---

[25] Woodhouse, *op. cit.*, Chapter IV.
[26] Anne R. Amory Parry, *Omens and Dreams in the Odyssey* (Radcliffe
thesis, 1957), p. 86.

There are several good arguments for this view of Athene and of the sea-tales, but a full discussion would not be relevant here. The important point, however, is that additional strong support for Amory's position can be found in the role played by Hermes in the *Odyssey*. For he is the god of the sea-tales, as Athene is the goddess of the Telemachy and the Ithacan adventure. It is Hermes who induces Calypso to let Odysseus go; it is Hermes who gives Odysseus the moly, and who advises him on how to deal with Circe (as with any enchantress); 'treat her rough, and don't trust her' is his masculine maxim. Although he appears only these two times, they are significant appearances, and on these occasions Odysseus receives more actual help from Hermes than he does from Athene in all her scenes put together. Why should Hermes be the god of the sea-tales? Because the sea-tales present life in a state of wild nature, and Hermes' rough-and-ready, practical 'cleverness' is better suited to this uncivilized world than is Athene's 'wisdom.' Athene's is city-wisdom, the knowledge of debate and counsel and kingly judgment—at its most superficial, her wisdom merges with tact and etiquette, and so she properly accompanies Telemachus on his Grand Tour of the polite Greek world. And why does Athene appear in Phaeacia, although Poseidon's enmity is supposed to follow Odysseus all the way to Ithaca? Because Phaeacia is civilized, because Odysseus has now left the world of nature and violence behind, and now has need of tact, eloquence and urbanity: Athene's wisdom.

Hermes, on the other hand, is feral, and suited to the wild world of giants and sorceresses and cannibals. He is the sly trickster, the god of native wit as well as the god of τέχνη, and these are the qualities the hero needs in his sea-adventures. It is, of course, a baser sort of wisdom than Athene's, more suitable for servants than for kings, but Odysseus the many-sided needs and has (at least by the end of the poem) both sorts. He can build a ship if necessary; he can handle women for his own purposes; he can even play the slave. As he says to Eumaeus (xv, 319-21), "By the favor of Hermes the Guide, who bestows grace and fame on the works of all men, there is no mortal who can compete with me at servants' work (δρηστοσύνη)." Hermes was also the patron of Odysseus' grandfather Autolycus, "the cleverest thief and liar of his day" (Book xix). If Athene is the divine representative of Odysseus' civilized wisdom (or total *sophia*, in Amory's opinion), Hermes represents his

natural 'wit,' his practical talents, his clever dishonesty and tricki-
ness, and just as Athene makes a final civilized settlement with the
suitors' kinsmen above ground, it is fitting that Hermes, in making
his final bow, should settle the suitors in their last resting place
below.

Now, what about the burial question? How can the suitors'
shades mingle with the properly buried dead? Page says,[27] "We
learn, to our intense annoyance, that the ghosts of the Suitors,
whose bodies are not yet buried or burnt, nevertheless enter Hades
without delay and mingle with other ghosts. Are we really required
to be so short of memory and so slow of wit?"

The dig about shortness of memory refers to the Elpenor episode,
which Page takes as theologically contradictory to the Nekuia.
However, it is Page who is short of memory; the Elpenor episode
actually says *nothing* about the unburied being kept at a distance;
Elpenor "comes up" from Erebus with the other souls, and he tells
Odysseus to bury him so that the gods will not turn against him,
Odysseus. His words imply that it is a terrible disgrace not to be
'wept and buried,' but that it has any practical consequences is
simply not stated. The evidence for this inflexible burial rule of
Page's, then, is to be found only in the *Iliad*. There we find, in Book
VII, 408-10, Agamemnon saying "I do not grudge the burning of
the bodies. For there is no refraining from giving them the peace of
a swift fire, once they have died." As in the Elpenor passage, swift
cremation or burial is seen here as a kindness and an honor, but the
reason why it is so is not stated. The explicit evidence is in fact
limited to *one scene only* (XXIII, 72-4), where the ghost of Patroclus
says "The shades, images of the dead, hold me apart, nor will they
let me mingle with them beyond the river, but I wander thus by
Hades' wide gates." Even in this passage there is the possibility
that no general rule is referred to; perhaps the shades consider
Patroclus' unburied state a particular disgrace; perhaps they let
other unburied men in or not as they please.

There is additional evidence that even in the *Iliad* non-burial
was generally considered as improper and disgraceful, but not as
an actual hindrance to the shade of the deceased. This evidence is
to be found in the gods' attitude toward Achilles' mistreatment of
Hector's body. Apollo had pity on Hector (XXIV, 20) "although he

---

[27] Page, *op. cit.*, p. 118.

was only a dead man (καὶ τεθνηότα περ)" Apollo speaks to the gods
(XXIV, 35-8)—"and now you won't save him, although he is only
a corpse (νέκυν περ ἐόντα), for his wife to look on and his mother
and his child and his father Priam and his people, who swiftly
would burn him in the fire and perform the funeral. . . . (54) In his
rage, he (Achilles) dishonors insensate earth. (κωφὴν δὴ γαῖαν)."
If Hector is unburied, then why is there so much emphasis on the
pointlessness of Achilles' act? If burial is an absolute prerequisite
for the peace of the shade, why does Apollo keep saying "only a
corpse," "*merely* a dead man?" Apollo and the other gods do not
say that Hector is being cruelly kept outside Hades' gates or beyond
the river; apparently their concern with his body is a question of
decency, not of theology. Hector's own father does not mention
any reason for wanting the body back other than to hold him in
his arms and to weep for him (XXIV, 227 and elsewhere).

Thus we find no more Homeric consistency in the reasons for
burial than we did about ways to the underworld and no more
consistency in the *Iliad* than in the *Odyssey*. As usual, literary motives seem to come first: Homer wanted this scene to take place
before the burial of the suitors, because the kinsmen were properly
to be dealt with last of all. And what Homer wanted, as usual,
he got.

Two aspects of the Nekuia still remain to be treated: first, Amphimedon's incorrect summary and second, the 'inferiority' and general superfluousness of the episode.

Amphimedon, according to his critics, makes two bad b'unders: he confuses the chronology of the weaving story, and he mistakenly implicates Penelope in the revenge plot. Now just how bad is the ghost's chronological memory? In his speech to Agamemnon, he says that Penelope's trick fooled the suitors for three years, and she was discovered at the beginning of the fourth (xxiv, 142) "ἀλλ' ὅτε τέτρατον ἦλθεν ἔτος καὶ ἐπήλυθον ὧραι / μηνῶν φθινόντων"—, and forced to complete the shroud. But when (εὖθ') she had finished and washed the robe, then (τότε δή) an evil daemon brought Odysseus to the swineherd's hut.

How does this account square with the facts given in the rest of the epic? The first reference to the weaving trick is in Book ii, where Antinoos tells the same story in the same words, up to the completion (but not the washing) of the robe. The web was finished, then, at least by the time of this speech at the beginning of the epic. The implication, according to some critics, is that it was completed long before this point: Antinoos is telling an anecdote about Penelope's duplicity in the past. This is an incorrect inference, however, since in the same speech Antinoos says that the suitors have been besieging Penelope for only three years, and it is now the fourth (ii, 89) "ἤδη γὰρ τρίτον ἐστὶν ἔτος, τάχα δ'εἶσι τέταρτον/ ἐξ οὗ ἀτέμβει θυμὸν ἐνὶ στήθεσσιν 'Αχαιῶν"). In other words, the period of their wooing exactly coincides with the period of the weaving trick, and the shroud has just now (in the beginning of the fourth year) been finished. So the length of time between the completion of the web and the arrival of Odysseus is the period between Book ii and Book xiii.

How long a delay is that? It has been frequently recognized that Homer had some difficulty in portraying simultaneous events—for example, the two councils of the gods in the beginning of the Odyssey seem to suggest that while Athene is visiting Telemachus, Hermes is at the same time disengaging Odysseus from Calypso. If this is so, then the delay between the completion of the web and the hero's return to Ithaca is not more than twenty-eight days. Odysseus takes five days to build his raft, sails for eighteen, is lost on the sea for three, spends two days with the Phaeacians and one day on the Phaeacian boat, and arrives home in the evening. Less than a month—or, if the two Olympian councils are not regarded as the same council, the time span is slightly more than a month. Surely this is not so long a time that Amphimedon is totally unjustified in saying "εὖθ'. . .τότε δή." In the context of Odysseus' years of absence and Penelope's drawn-out anxiety, a month would seem negligible. Once the question of her remarrying was settled, Penelope would certainly have been given at least a month's grace to make her final decision on *whom* to marry. Just as the weaving plot demands (to be artistically satisfying), the deliverer does arrive in the nick of time.

The heroine herself confirms Amphimedon's view of the chronology. In Book xix, she tells the disguised Odysseus the story of her weaving trick—and after the familiar line "I was forced to complete it, unwillingly" ("ἐξετέλεσσα, καὶ οὐκ ἐθέλουσ', ὑπ' ἀνάγκης"), she says "*And now* I can neither escape this marriage nor find any other trick" ("νῦν δ'οὔτ' ἐκφυγέειν δύναμαι γάμον οὔτε τιν' ἄλλην/ μῆτιν ἔθ' εὑρίσκω"). So it is clear that she, like Amphimedon, considers that the weaving device has just now failed, and that the critical aftermath of its failure is in the immediate present.

Amphimedon does, however, make a real mistake, about Penelope's role in the final event: he says (xxiv, 167-8) "αὐτὰρ ὁ ἥν ἄλοχον πολυκερδείῃσιν ἄνωγε/τόξον μνηστήρεσσι θέμεν πολιόν τε σίδηρον . . . ." "He (Odysseus) in his cunning ordered his wife to set up for the suitors the bow and the grey iron. . ." As we know from Book xix, Penelope herself devised the trial of the bow. The disguised Odysseus encouraged her not to delay it, but she did not know her husband, and had no knowledge that what she was doing would fit in with his plans; in xxi, she fetched the bow on inspiration from Athene. Amphimedon's story, a more convincingly motivated version than was the actual sequence of events, implies that Penelope had already recognized her husband and was in on the revenge plot. The simplest (and perhaps the best) explanation of this error is Lang's:[1] "This is merely an erroneous inference of the

---

[1] Lang, *Homer and the Epic*, p. 317.

ghost's." How could Amphimedon think otherwise?[2] Penelope certainly behaved as if she were in on the plot. Although erroneous, Amphimedon's inference is certainly natural enough—otherwise, Penelope's action is incomprehensible and unmotivated. Actually, it was unmotivated—Athene's prompting being, as Woodhouse has seen, a convenient shorthand for "spontaneously, for no reason." As Woodhouse points out,[3] Homer had a difficult problem at this point in the story; if Penelope recognized Odysseus before the suitors are dealt with, her behavior preceding the revenge can be made convincing, but the recognition scene between husband and wife—a high point of the epic—will be robbed of dramatic power. Apparently Homer preferred to save the recognition and reunion for the choicer dramatic moment, after the revenge; he was therefore faced with the dilemma of an ignorant, unmotivated Penelope. He patched it up as well as possible by having her consciously behave as if she knew the truth (as Amory points out),[4] but not without some sacrifice of psychological 'realism.'

Amphimedon's error, then, is a natural one—his version implies a less dramatically effective plot than Homer's, but a more convincing one. But why did Homer allow one of his characters thus to point up the psychological flaw in his story? Perhaps it is a slip-up on the poet's part—an unconscious reversion (as Woodhouse and Page think) [5] to an earlier or better-known form of the tale. Or perhaps Homer assumed that by this time his audience would have forgotten the precise details of the revenge story and would accept this more realistic plot as a correct summary; in this way, the bard would eat his cake and have it, too: his hearers would remember the striking husband-wife recognition scene, but would fail to notice its incompatibility with the also striking and clever revenge plot as recapitulated by Amphimedon.

But this is merely speculation. Whatever Homer's reasons for allowing Amphimedon to blunder, the more important (and often neglected) fact is how much Amphimedon got *right*. It is a long

---

[2] Homer is generally careful not to attribute the omniscience of the bard to his human characters: cf. xii, 389-90 where he painstakingly provides a rational explanation for how Odysseus came to know of a dialogue on Olympus.

[3] Woodhouse, *Composition*, Chapter XV.

[4] Amory, *Omens and Dreams*, p. 173. Also cf. P. W. Harsch, "Penelope and Odysseus in *Odyssey* XIX," *AJP* 71 (1950), pp. 1-21.

[5] Woodhouse, *op.cit.*, p. 70; Page, *Homeric Odyssey*, pp. 121-8.

and detailed epitome, so detailed that it is hard to imagine that it could have been written by someone who was not exceedingly familiar with our *Odyssey*. There probably were other versions of the Return of Odysseus current in and before and after Homer's time, but is it likely that any of them contained this precise combination: Odysseus arrives in Ithaca, stays in swineherd's cabin; Telemachus returns to palace first; Eumaeus and Odysseus follow later, Odysseus dressed as a beggar, *and*, Antinoos is the first suitor felled?

No. It is not likely. This speech seems to have been written, whether or not by Homer, for *this version* of the *Odyssey*. Why, then, should any critic worry about the mistake (or mistakes, if the web story is still considered incorrect) that Amphimedon made? The only anti-Homeric argument based on this mistake is that the author of this speech must have been epitomizing a different *Odyssey*; if we grant that Amphimedon's speech was written specifically for *our Odyssey*, then the case against Homeric authorship collapses. (That Homer would be more familiar with his own material than a forger would be is an unprovable assumption—it can be argued with equal persuasiveness that a forger or a rhapsode would be more careful not to make mistakes.)

As has been mentioned before, Amphimedon's epitome is the third of three, and completes the summarizing of the entire plot of the *Odyssey*. Telemachus summarizes his adventures for Penelope; Odysseus summarizes the sea-tales in xxiii and in Amphimedon's speech the poet reviews the last and most fundamental part of the three-fold plot, the Return and Revenge of Odysseus.

The fifth and final objection to the Nekuia is that it is pointless. It interrupts the plot, contributes nothing, and is poorly written.

I cannot, of course, prove that the Nekuia is well written. Those who dislike it will probably continue to dislike it no matter what anyone says on behalf of the episode. I do trust, however, that the large number of lines here repeated from other parts of the epic no longer constitutes a major threat to the episode's acceptance. Shewan has gone into this point at great length:[6] "Knowing the epic way," he concludes, "we expect many pieces of description to recur in the *ipsissima verba* used earlier in the book." In this I concur, and trust that it would be superfluous on my part to add

---

[6] Shewan, 'Continuation', 41.

anything more; most critics these days recognize, I think, that formulaic repetitions are not only excusable in Homer, they are to be expected.

What I can and will argue about, however, is the relevance of the Nekuia to the rest of the *Odyssey*. The episode does not interrupt the plot; it complements, contributes to, and helps to complete the story of Odysseus' return in at least four ways.

First of all, as has been pointed out frequently, Penelope here gets her long overdue encomium. She is, after all, the heroine of the *Odyssey*; the most important of the three plots depends on and revolves around her, and her proverbial constancy and 'wisdom' are necessary to the happy resolution of the hero's adventures. But until this point in the story she has received no word of praise for her part in the revenge plot, no proper panegyric for her long years of faithfulness, unless we count Anticleia's few words in the underworld. Penelope's praise is particularly satisfying, therefore, when it does come, at this late point and from this particular character. For Agamemnon is not only dead, and therefore presumably more respectable and objective as a judge than Odysseus would have been, but he is also (understandably) a considerable misogynist, who in the eleventh book had called women an untrustworthy lot, and had warned Odysseus to be wary of Penelope on his return. His suspicions now quelled, the hero of Troy ungrudgingly gives Penelope her due: the gods themselves will inspire songs in her honor; her virtue will become as proverbial as Clytaemnestra's faithlessness. How much more pleasing this one late burst of admiration is than, for example, the rather wearying outpourings of the *Alcestis*, which actually diminish that heroine's stature by their excessiveness.

The second useful function the Nekuia serves is to provide a funeral. Perhaps every proper epic of Homer's time included one; we have no evidence on this point. (Although Lord considers laments and funerals to have a special importance in epic poetry generally.) [7] More important, however, is the fact that the *Iliad* does contain an important one, and the *Odyssey*, although its subject matter and general approach are very different from the *Iliad*, in several respects echoes that work almost reverently. For example, the games: in the *Iliad*, the funeral games of Patroclus,

---

[7] A. B. Lord, in: Wace and Stubbings, *Companion to Homer* (London, 1962), p. 202.

although they are dealt with in such loving (and to moderns, excessive) detail, still come at a natural point in the plot. But the Phaeacian games are really dragged in; presumably they were introduced (like many of the epic's sacrifices, displays of *techne*, and descriptions of clothing, etc.) either as an epic convention, an already established feature of the poem which the audience would expect, or simply because the *Iliad* too had its games. Might not the funeral here described fill a similar function, to entertain an audience already familiar with and enthusiastic about (or even reverent towards) the *Iliad*?

As far as funerals go, however, the poet of the *Odyssey* had a problem: Elpenor was too insignificant a character (compared with Patroclus) to rate a really impressive rite; the suitors were villains; and Odysseus himself was not to die in the course of the story. So—if the epic was to contain a hero's funeral to equal or surpass that of the *Iliad*, it would have to belong to a character peripheral to the story—and what better choice than the very hero of the *Iliad*, whose final end had been foreseen but not described in that epic? The story of Achilles is not really complete until this moment; as Sainte-Beuve remarked,[8] "Homère a esquissé en traits sublimes ce que furent ces funerailles, ce qu'elles durent être; la fin de l'Odyssée repond ainsi a la pensée même de l'Iliade, et y concorde par un effet plein de grandeur."

We have seen that the Nekuia provides a last bow for Hermes, and for Achilles. It is also a farewell appearance of the suitors, and of Agamemnon, Patroclus, Antilochus, and Ajax. Thus the whole Trojan story is completed in the *Odyssey*; as Bassett says,[9] "every prominent Greek whose story was left unfinished in the *Iliad* finds a place either in the Telemachy or in one of the two Necyias." And what of the characters of the *Odyssey*? Penelope and Eurycleia appeared for the last time just before this scene; the rest of the major characters (Odysseus, Telemachus, Laertes, the two herds, Mentor, and Athene herself) have their curtain calls at the very end; two living men, however, played important parts in the plot, and cannot reasonably appear in Ithaca—Nestor and Menelaus. But they, too, have final bows: in Agamemnon's descrip-

---

[8] Sainte-Beuve, *Étude sur Quintus Smyrnaeus*, p. 385, quoted in Lang, *op. cit.*, p. 317.

[9] Bassett, *The Poetry of Homer* (Berkeley, 1932), p. 175.

tion of Achilles' funeral, Nestor is described as preventing a panic among the troops, who were terrified at the arrival of Thetis and her nymphs. Nestor is singled out for praise, called "the man who knew many ancient things, Nestor, whose counsels had prevailed (often) before this" (51-2). Menelaus, too, is brought into the narrative; Agamemnon reminds Amphimedon of the occasion on which he and Menelaus visited Ithaca. Perfunctory though they are, these references seem to have been worked in deliberately by a poet who was trying to get into the concluding scenes of his epic some mention of every major figure who has taken part in the story. (To be *really* complete, of course, we would have to consider the conclusion of the epic as beginning with the Odysseus-Penelope reconciliation, where Helen is mentioned, or at least with Odysseus' epitome of his wanderings, which lists the chief characters in that part of the story. But this would perhaps be stretching a point.)

At last we come to that function of the episode which seems to be both the most obvious and the most important: the comparison of Odysseus with Agamemnon and Achilles. Character-comparison is a technique which pervades the entire *Odyssey*; nearly every character in the poem can be compared with or contrasted to either Odysseus, or Penelope, or Telemachus. This point will be discussed more fully in Chapter Six; for now, let us limit the examination to Achilles and Agamemnon. Agamemnon's case is the simpler; it has been repeatedly recognized that his tragedy had a special fascination for the poet of the *Odyssey*; it is referred to some nine times in the poem. The poet's reason for making so much of Agamemnon's story is twofold. First, during the course of the poem, he includes descriptions of the *nostoi* of all the major Trojan heroes, and this one is the most dramatic.

Second, the story is admirably suited for comparison with the story of Odysseus' return, as has been pointed out by D'Arms and Hulley, Post, and others.[10] The analogy is on more than one occasion made explicit: in Book i, 298-302, for example, Athene exhorts Telemachus to be as brave as Orestes; in iii the same comparison is made by Nestor; in xi, Agamemnon contrasts Penelope and Clytaemnestra, and, even more interestingly, contrasts Odysseus'

---

[10] Edward F. D'Arms and Karl K. Hulley, "The Oresteia-Story in the *Odyssey*," *Trans. Phil. As.* 77 (1946), *passim*; L. A. Post, "The Moral Pattern in Homer," *Trans. Phil. As.* 70 (1939), pp. 158-190.

future reunion with his son to his own homecoming, in which he was deprived of the sight of *his* son. Why does Agamemnon make such a point of this, acting as if Clytaemnestra's greatest crime had been, not the double murder nor her adultery, but that she deprived him of a last sight of Orestes ?Because the father-son relationship is the most important bond in the *Odyssey*; Odysseus' supreme success, to Homer, consists more in his possession of a good son, and secondarily of a good wife, than in his own heroism. The less attractive qualities of Agamemnon—seen so clearly in the *Iliad*—are entirely played down in the *Odyssey*, to make the comparison with Odysseus simple and clear.

The analogy is almost excessively straightforward: the evil Clytaemnestra is the opposite of the virtuous Penelope; Aegisthus is the same as the suitors (see i, 32-43)—although clearly warned, he brought about his own downfall through his own wickedness; Orestes is the same as Telemachus—he was a good son, who performed a courageous act of revenge; and finally, Agamemnon is the opposite of Odysseus—the latter lived most of his life with supreme success (xxiv, 24-5 "Son of Atreus, we used to say that you, of all our heroes, were the favorite for all time of Zeus the Thunderer") but fell in deepest tragedy, while the former, although he seemed ill-starred beyond all justice (e.g. xi, 216, "My child, unluckiest of mortals—"), was fated to end his sufferings in supreme success. And what does the Nekuia contribute to this pattern? Agamemnon's eulogy makes the comparison explicit and final; the story of Odysseus was not complete at the time of the other references to Agamemnon's tragedy; the question of Penelope's trustworthiness was not yet settled, Telemachus had not yet proved himself, and the suitors were still unpunished. But now, in the house of Hades, it is all over: justice has been done, the virtuous can be recognized, and the analogy—first brought up in Book i—is complete. It may perhaps be argued that this hammering-home of an already simple analogy is unnecessary and not very illuminating, but such a criticism would amount to a criticism of Homer himself, not of the Nekuia; the *Odyssey* is not a morally ambiguous tale like the *Iliad*; it is a melodrama in which heroes and villains are clearly defined, and to expect such a moralistic story not to drive its moral home is to ask for a different story altogether.

But what about Achilles? Unlike Agamemnon, his end was

glorious. In the Nekuia, his splendid funeral is described at great length, and Agamemnon explicitly compares the hero's 'blessedness' with his own misfortune. (36) "ὄλβιε Πηλέος υἰέ, θεοῖς ἐπιείκελ' Ἀχιλλεῦ"—"Blessed son of Peleus, Achilles like to the gods—" says Agamemnon; a few speeches later he echoes those words with (192) "ὄλβιε Λαέρταο πάι, πολυμήχαν' Ὀδυσσεῦ—" "Blessed son of Laertes, resourceful Odysseus." The comparison is clear; Achilles and Odysseus are alike in their happiness, in contrast to Agamemnon. Is one preferable to the other? Since Odysseus is listed second, there is perhaps an implication that his fortunes outshine those of the *Iliad*'s hero. There is no denying that "θεοῖς ἐπιείκελ'" Achilles is, in a sense, more divine, more brilliant than this "πολυμή-χαν'" "resourceful" human competitor, but so far as this poem is concerned, this contrast may also be in Odysseus' favor. In the rest of the poem, implied comparisons between Achilles and Odysseus can be detected in a number of instances, and (as opposed to the comparisons between Odysseus and Agamemnon, which are in terms of final success and domestic felicity) these comparisons are in terms of character, or rather, style of life.

For the famous Choice of Achilles was offered to Odysseus, too, as it is to every man. The decision which the hero of the *Iliad* made—for death and glory—is the simpler of the two ways. Telemachus (i, 237-40) mentions this possibility with envy: If Odysseus had died at Troy, he says, he would have had a splendid funeral and would have left me great glory to inherit. Odysseus himself echoes this sentiment in v (306, 311): "Thrice blessed, four times," he says, "were the Danaans who died on the broad fields of Troy . . . would that I had died there . . . I would have had my burial rites, and the Achaeans would have spread my fame . . . ." But as it is, Odysseus' lot—determined by his character—is not to die brilliantly in battle; his lot is to endure. He is not so glorious as Achilles, but he has patience, which Achilles did not have; he is flexible and resourceful, and he endures. He is not semi-divine, like Achilles, but he is a man better equipped to deal with this world. Further, he *likes* this world; in the Calypso episode, he deliberately rejects divinity and embraces humanity with all its imperfections— Penelope is inferior to Calypso in beauty and stature, but the hero chooses her nonetheless; he is unashamed of his domesticity.

And is not this choice offered by Calypso practically identical with the more famous choice of Achilles? It is a question of divinity versus humanity, and Odysseus unhesitatingly makes a decision opposite to that of Achilles.

The two heroes had already been contrasted, and in the same way, in the *Iliad*. When Achilles wants to rush into battle at the climactic point of the epic (Book xix), the practical Odysseus restrains him. You are mightier than I, says Odysseus, but I am wiser than you; the army must eat first. This scene points up very nicely the difference between the two heroes—in it the whole character study of the *Odyssey* is already present in miniature. Achilles can do without food and drink, because he is scarcely human; Odysseus operates on a lower plane—he is the sort of man who can do servants' work and act the buffoon if it will serve his purpose—but, in the affairs of the world, he is right and Achilles is wrong; he speaks correctly when he says, "you are mightier but I am wiser."

In the poet's final evaluation, however, is Odysseus' kind of heroism actually seen as *better* than that of Achilles? Or are they (in the *Odyssey*) merely seen as two different ways of life, equally likely to produce final blessedness? Book xi seems to me to indicate Homer's bias. In his interview with the shade of Achilles, Odysseus says (483-6) "No man has ever been or will ever be more blessed than you. For while you were living the Argives honored you as a god, and now you are the mighty ruler of the dead down here." But Achilles impatiently denies this flattering tribute; I would rather be slave to a pauper on earth, he says, than king of all these corpses . . . but tell me about my son, and my father . . . . The order of these statements makes Homer's point clear. I think, Life itself is the most important thing; a glorious funeral is less to be desired than a fine son; Odysseus' human domesticity and self-preservation are better in the end than Achilles' divinity and glorious death. It is not, perhaps, a very noble point of view—but it is a lucid and sensible one, and just what we might expect from a bard who was able to find in the herding of pigs and the washing of dirty robes the stuff of poetry.

The second Nekuia is, of course, a doublet—we have already had one underworld scene—and this fact is the basis for some rather old-fashioned objections to the episode. But the *Odyssey* abounds in doublets: there are two cannibalism episodes; Calypso and Circe are somewhat similar; Leukothea and Eidothea are almost identical, and so on. The poet of the *Odyssey* apparently did not mind telling a good story twice, any more than he minded repeating a good turn of phrase. And in some of these doublets there is a significant difference, for example, in the two cannibalism episodes. In the Cyclops story, it is Odysseus' rashness (first in staying to explore the cave and meet its owner, next in boasting at the end of the scene) which brings trouble. In the Laestrygonian story, however, Odysseus shows that he has learned something about caution; he warily keeps his ship outside the cove while the others sail in; they are lost, and only his ship escapes. The two underworld scenes show a similar progress in knowledge; in the first, Agamemnon has learned the truth, and the hero of the *Odyssey* is found comparable to the hero of the *Iliad*.

The second Nekuia, then, serves at least five functions. It provides the third of three epitomes, which among them summarize the entire *Odyssey*. It provides an impressive panegyric for Penelope, who up till this point has not been properly rewarded. It provides the description of a funeral, which may have been a convention in *all* epics, or may simply be an echo of the *Iliad*. It provides a last bow for several major characters of the *Iliad* and the *Odyssey*: Hermes, the suitors, Achilles, Agamemnon, Menelaus, and Nestor. And it provides Homer's final evaluation of his hero, in comparison with Agamemnon and Achilles, the two chief characters of the *Iliad*. The scene may still be called poor, of course, but how can it be called irrelevant?

VI. THE LAERTES SCENE

While the shades converse in the house of Hades, Odysseus and his party make their way to the well-kept farm of Laertes. For a tantalizing interval the hero withholds his identity from the old man, but finally taking pity, he reveals himself and proves who he is by naming the trees and vines Laertes had given him when he was a child. With the aid of Athene and a bath, Laertes' appearance improves immeasurably, and father and son then meet Telemachus and the herds for a festive lunch, in which they are joined by the old servant Dolius and his six sons.

The major objections to the Laertes scene are as follows: 1. There are linguistic differences. Denys Page rejects the episode chiefly on this basis;[1] in fact, this is the only scene of the conclusion which he finds objectionable philologically. 2. There is a problem about Laertes, urged by G. S. Kirk and by M. I. Finley— [2] 'the fine and well-tilled farm of Laertes' (205-6) is inconsistent, they feel, with the pathetic picture of Laertes given in Book i. "It is in this book, too, that we have the only explicit reference to Laertes' ever having been king," says Finley. 3. The prominent part played by Dolius at this late date seems inexplicable, in view of the negligible, shadowy, and inconsistent role he has played heretofore in the epic. 4. Odysseus' teasing of his pathetic old father is cruel; the scene is in bad taste and presents our hero in an unappealing role.

As usual, I shall examine these objections in order. The first is the linguistic argument. A detailed examination of the language of the whole conclusion is not within the scope of this study; Page, however, has reserved one of his nastiest dicta for those who make light of the linguistic objections: "I suppress the names of those who have written such falsehood as the following: 'The evidence is, as regards both language and metre, so slight as to be negligible'; 'Language and metre, then, furnish no good evidence even for suspecting that 23:297 to the end of 24 could not have come directly from Homer's hand.' It needs hardly to be said that the

---

[1] Page, *Homeric Odyssey*, p. 104.

[2] Kirk, *Songs of Homer*, p. 250; M. I. Finley, *The World of Odysseus* (New York, 1954), p. 90.

writers had not taken the trouble to find out what the evidence is." [3]

In view of this judicious and gentlemanly statement, it seems advisable to digress briefly on the linguistic evidence against the Laertes episode, lest the thunderings of Pagean rhetoric lead us into an unreasoning terror of nothing more than *quae pueri in tenebris pavitant finguntque futura.*

No part of the *Odyssey*, admits Page, is entirely free from verbal and syntactic 'abnormalities,' and of the four episodes of the Continuation, only the Laertes scene is unusual. But there, he says, "the evidence is indeed overwhelming, and leaves no room whatever for doubt: that scene as a whole was composed by a poet familiar with the idioms, syntax and vocabulary of an era not earlier than the sixth century B.C.; a poet whose understanding of the older Epic language and versification is very imperfect." [4]

The list of specific objections which follows is indeed, at first glance, most impressive: for 207 lines of text Page cites 32 'errors.' As I will endeavor to show later, there are several plausible historical explanations for this formidable array of irregularities, even if Page is entirely correct about every one of them. However, there is a fair chance that he is in fact *not* correct about most of them: at least twenty-two of the thirty-two seem to me to be probable or possible errors of Page rather than of Homer.[5] Let us review these twenty-two briefly:[6]

1. line 237, εἰπεῖν ὡς ἔλθοι: a late grammatical use, according to Page, but explained by L. R. Palmer [7] as an indirect question, not an indirect statement, and thus perfectly regular for Homer.

2. l. 242, κατέχων κεφαλήν: explained by Van der Valk,[8] who gives two similar examples, as a type of expression characteristic of the poet of the *Odyssey*.

---

[3] Page, *op. cit.*, p. 111.

[4] *Ibid.*, p. 102.

[5] I must admit, and it is perhaps obvious, that I am not a specialist in linguistics. For a more thorough treatment of Page's data, I refer the reader to H. Erbse's excellent book. And of course he should also consult P. Chantraine, *Grammaire Homérique* (Paris, 1953, 1958) and G. P. Shipp, *Studies in the Language of Homer* (Cambridge, 1972). I regret that John Finley's new study of the *Odyssey* appeared too late for me to use it.

[6] All the following quotations from Page are in *op. cit.*, pp. 104-109.

[7] L. R. Palmer, "The Language of Homer", in Wace and Stubbings, p. 158.

[8] Van der Valk, *Textual Criticism*, pp. 52-53.

3. l. 245, εὖ τοι κομιδὴ ἔχει: Page calls this an "idiom of later Greek," but there is no need to understand this expression as an idiom, and κομιδή as "care" is a specifically *Homeric*, not a late, word.

4. l. 247, οὐκ ὄγχνη οὐ πρασιή: This synizesis is not clearly irregular; Page himself cites four other Homeric examples.

5. l. 250, αὐχμεῖς: "αὐχμεῖν and its cognates are foreign to the Homeric poems," says Page, but this is an argument from silence, about a rather unusual word.

6. l. 251, ἀεργίης: a perfectly regular formation from ἀεργός (like, as Page himself admits, κακοεργίη in Od. 22.374.) [9]

7. l. 252, δούλειον: another argument from Homeric silence. Found in cognate forms six times in Homer. It is a peculiar fact that Homer did not make more use of the δοῦλος words, but that fact does not impugn this passage, as Homer clearly *knew* the stem δουλ-, and δοῦλος itself (though not used by Homer) is found on the Pylos tablets. Eibse demonstrates that the -ειος termination has good parallels, but Shipp (p. 362) says it is a Doric formation.

8. l. 252, ἐπιπρέπει: another argument from silence. This is a perfectly ordinary Homeric formation; e.g. μεταπρέπω is a favorite compound in Homer.

9. l. 252, ἀρτίφρων: Page says that in the Homeric poems, "αρτι-compounds are very rare." But they are rare also in later Greek literature, if we distinguish between later compounds formed from ἄρτι, "just, newly," which Homer does not use, and those formed from ἄρτιος, "complete, sound," which he does use. ἀρτίφρων is clearly of the latter type, similar to the 'rare' but characteristically Homeric ἀρτιεπής and ἄρτιπος.

10. l. 268, φιλίων: an interesting example of Page's methods. Our critic reaches the height of his courtroom style on this rather tenuous objection; beginning with an "It is obvious that—" he goes on to call his opponents "contortionists," and concludes his note with a resounding "no Greek ever repeated this blunder." The gist of his argument, restated somewhat less passionately, is this: the author of l. 268 has used φιλίων as the nom. sing. comparative of φίλος. This, according to Page, is an impossible, un-Greek

---

[9] I am grateful to the editors of Mnemosyne for pointing out that ἀεργίης (with long iota) can also represent ἀεγείης. This is a regular derivation from * ἀ-Ϝεργής, a conpound that is paralleled by Mycenean ke-re-si-jo we-ke ΚρησιοϜερὴς.

formation, an imitation based on a misreading of 19.350 ff, where φιλίων is "obviously" not a comparative adjective, but the gen. pl. of φίλιος (which adjective Page admits does not appear in Homer.) The major problem about this argument is that a number of people (e.g. Butcher and Lang, and G. H. Palmer in their translations, and Liddell and Scott—the "contortionists" of whom Page speaks) disagree with Page's reading of the crucial lines in xix, and think that there as in xxiv Homer formed the comparative of φίλος like that of κακός. I would urge that their reading of xix 351 is correct on the following grounds: the whole section (of which Page does not quote the important first words) reads, "ξεῖνε φίλ' οὐ γάρ πώ τις ἀνὴρ πεπνυμένος ὧδε/ξείνων τηλεδαπῶν φιλίων ἐμὸν ἵκετο δῶμα..." "*Dear* stranger," begins Penelope, addressing the disguised Odysseus—and then she finds it necessary to explain her sudden use of this affectionate word "φίλ'"—"(I say this) *because* no stranger so wise has ever come to my house *more dear*—" Penelope is not in the habit of calling strange beggars 'Dear'; until this point in the interview she has limited herself to the severe "ξεῖνε," which she has used six times. Now, however, her testing of the stranger is over; she is satisfied that he is no imposter (and perhaps suspects that he is Odysseus himself), and she spontaneously uses an intimate form of address. The γάρ which follows indicates that her next words will give parenthetically her reason for using the word "φίλ'." Page's reading, "no man so wise has ever come to my house," neglects the logical structure of the sentence and of the entire interview.

11. 1. 273, ξεινήια: Page's comment is "our poet was unaware that ξεινήιον is established in use in the epic as a substantive, not as an adjective." But ξεινήια as an adjective with δῶρα is clearly the older, fuller form for which the substantive ξεινήια is an abbreviation; it seems therefore unlikely to have been the contribution of the late, ignorant Athenian whom Page urges on us as the author of the episode. Also, like "our poet," I was unaware that Homer had "established" any list of officially approved forms. Erbse (p. 210) thinks, however, that the word is used here as a substantive, in apposition with δῶρα. He cites several parallels.

12. 1. 286, ξενίη: occurs also in 1. 314. ξεν- for ξείν- occurs several times in the earlier books of the *Odyssey*, though not in the *Iliad*; the formation seems therefore unobjectionable.

13. and 14. ll. 319 and 320, προΰτυψε and ἐπιάλμενος: Page

finds these words (although Homeric) 'insensitive' and 'unsuitable.' Like Aristarchus, he would presumably like to excise any Homeric expressions which seem to him excessively vivid or vigorous. It is a matter of taste. But the fact remains that there is no linguistic objection to these words.

15. l. 341, ὀνόμηνας: ὀνομαίνω is a fairly common Homeric word, usually meaning 'repeat,' 'name,' or 'say.' Here, to be sure, it is used with an implication of promising, but naming is also implied. Shipp (p. 362) cites two examples with similar meaning from the *Iliad*. Perhaps the use with future infinitive is a bit odd, but the sense is clear and the form ὀνομαίνω definitely not "remote from the old Epic."

16. l. 342, διατρύγιος: Page's only comment is "His διατρύγιος is, as one might hope, unique." It is not, however, entirely clear why 'one might hope' this; διατρύγιος is a seed-catalogue sort of word, presumably of limited usefulness in philosophy, history, tragedy, and so on, which would explain its absence from other Greek literature, but no doubt extremely useful in the daily converse of the grape-grower. Analogously, the English word "everbearing" does not find a place in Webster's New Collegiate Dictionary, but anyone who cultivates strawberries knows and uses the word. Much circumlocution would be needed if "everbearing" did not exist, and διατρύγιος is a useful word of exactly the same kind. That in Homer's time there were some grape varieties with the characteristic of bearing continuously throughout the summer is indicated by vii, 122 ff. The δια—is, however, odd.

17. l. 343, ἥην: this word, which Page calls "another monster," occurs several other times in Homer, and *only* in Homer. It is hard, then, to see how it can possibly be evidence for late authorship.

18. l. 343, ἀνά: the adverbial use without tmesis is rare, but can be found in *Iliad* XVIII, 562, in a sentence which, interestingly enough, is also about vines. It is certainly not a 'late' or Attic usage, and therefore, like the previous example, does not seem to give much help to Page's case.

19. l. 360, προὔπεμψ': occurs contracted also in *Iliad* VIII, 357 *Odyssey* xxi, 354, etc., but perhaps Page and others are right in 'correcting' these. Perhaps, too, they are wrong. Erbse (p. 217) cites good parallels.

20. l. 388, ἐξ ἔργων μογέοντες: a logical usage. There is room for argument (and there *is* argument) as to whether μογεῖν means

"to be tired out" in any of the other Homeric examples; in any case, the word itself is commoner in Homer than in later literature.

21. l. 394, θάμβευς: a late Ionic form; however, Palmer suggests that it should be written -εος (as should θέρευς, *Odyssey* vii, 118) and scanned with synizesis.[10]

22. l. 402, οὖλέ τε καὶ μέγα χαῖρε: οὖλε is presumably from οὖλος,= (ὅλϜος whole, sound; οὖλε= *salve*); this phrase, which recurs in the Hymn to Apollo but not later, certainly looks like an *ancient* formula, not a late invention.

Thus the formidable list is not so formidable after all. And what of the ten objections which remain? The first, l. 240, ἐπέεσσιν πειρηθῆναι, is a metrical irregularity; the second, l. 279, εἰδαλίμας, is a neologism which recurs only once in later literature; the third, l. 286, ὑπάρξῃ, does seem like an error, being a common word of later Attic. ποστὸν (l. 288) is found only three times more in Greek literature; how then can Page call it 'very late' and 'apparently Attic'?; the preponderance of 'late' (i.e. post-Homeric) and Attic literature in our totality of Greek texts would seem to make it more likely for any rare word to appear in that dialect than in some other. δαὶ (l. 299) does seem clearly an error; but there are other readings in the ms. The grammatical construction of ll. 343-4 is difficult indeed; it is hard to see, however, what conclusion about authorship can be drawn from this difficulty. ἀποψύχοντα (l. 348) *does* look wrong, as do δείπνῳ ἐπεχείρεον (386) and ἀπεκλελάθεσθε (394). (Of the latter it may be said that ἀπεκ- compounds are so late and rate—post-classical—as to suggest scribal error.) The last example, 'Οδυσσεῦς (l. 398), is rather peculiar and probably incorrect, but, again, not very convincing proof for 6th century Attic authorship.

The logical problem is this: even if the majority of Page's objections are entirely well-founded (including those which we have considered unlikely), they do not furnish any substantial evidence for what Page purports to prove, that the author of the Laertes section was 'late' and probably an Athenian. The most they could logically indicate is that this section is peculiarly dotted with rare words and errors. This situation would seem to pose as great a logical problem for Page as for us: how does he explain the lin-

---

[10] Palmer, *op. cit.*, p. 109.

guistic discrepancy between this episode and the rest of the 'Continuation,' which he considers also to be a product of the sixth century, and presumably composed by the same forger? How did the forger manage to write acceptable Homeric Greek for the *Nekuia* and Battle episodes, and then lapse into ignorant Attic lateness only in *this* section? Page does not furnish any explanation for this anomaly; since he has other sorts of objections to the three other episodes, he is content to lump all four together as spurious, each component part being rejected on whatever grounds seem handiest.

If verbal differences do exist between the Laertes episode and the rest of the conclusion, can *we* furnish any logical explanations for them? Yes, there are several historical possibilities to account for the situation:

1. In this episode Homer may have been borrowing extensively from another (earlier or contemporary) written work.

2. This scene may have been composed or revised by Homer later than the rest of the *Odyssey*. If we assume (as we did in Chapter Two) that the poet either (a) wrote down his own work or (b) dictated it to a literate friend, son, or disciple, the setting down of the entire text may have extended over a relatively long period, with revisions (or carelessness) particularly likely to occur in the concluding portions of the work. There may also have been a change of amanuensis at various points.

3. A certain number of these errors are undoubtedly scribal errors. Why should this section contain more scribal errors than the preceding and following scenes? There are numerous possibilities: perhaps the scribe was tired when he came to this episode; perhaps these pages were mutilated by some accident, and so forth.

4. Some of these errors may be one-word interpolations. Precisely because this is a good and typically Homeric scene, an important and well-written set piece, it may have been particularly subject to tampering and 'modernization' by a) a rhapsode who wished to perform it by itself or b) a schoolmaster who was setting a particular exercise.

In presenting these logical possibilities, I do not wish to imply that all work on Homeric language is vain, but merely that it is not decisive. Historically the linguistic arguments have carried more weight than that to which they are logically entitled, even if they are correct in every detail. There is an aura of Science and Clearheadedness around word-counting which is perhaps real in the case of the Federalist Papers investigation (where the documentary material was massive and the language well known) but seems illusory in the case of criticism of two poems written (or sung or dictated) by an unknown author (or authors) at an uncertain date (or dates) in an artificial and internally inconsistent dialect of an ancient and imperfectly understood language. As Carroll Moulton says in a clear-headed article "the list of irregular expressions hardly amounts to overwhelming evidence in favor of condemning 623 lines." [11]

By all means, then, scholars must continue to pay attention to the language of Homer, but until such time as our philological data are unassailable enough to be entrusted to an IBM programmer, we will also have to pay attention to archaeology, to plot structure, to apparent meaning, to literary technique, and to whatever logic we can find in our own imperfect brains. Let us, accordingly, press on to the second (Moses Finley's) objection to the Laertes episode, that it presents a pretty picture of Laertes and his farm which is discordant with the rest of the *Odyssey*.

This criticism can be disposed of rather rapidly. The picture of Laertes given in Book i, and also in ii, iv, xi, xv and xvi, is *entirely* consistent with xxiv. In xxiv, Odysseus explicitly contrasts the fine and prosperous state of the farm with the ragged and disreputable condition of the old man himself. The same contrast is maintained throughout the epic: in i, Athene says that Laertes never comes to town, and lives a life of suffering on his farm, with only an old woman caring for him. This is a pitiful picture, but there is no implication that Laertes' misery or solitude is due to poverty; on the contrary, it is clear that his hibernation and hard physical labor are of his own choosing; they reflect not his status in Ithaca but his state of mind. In iv, Eurycleia assures Penelope that one of the Arkeisian line will always hold "the lofty halls and the fat fields far off" (754-7)—the same fields, presumably, which Odysseus finds so admirable in xxiv. In xi, Anticleia tells Odysseus that the estate is still intact. As for Laertes, however, she paints a pathetic picture of senility: he stays on the farm, has given up

---

[11] Carrol Moulton, "The End of the Odyssey", *GRBS* 15, 2, (1974), p. 160.

sleeping in beds. Dressed in rags, he curls up in the dust by the fire
in the winter, and in summer sleeps outdoors on a pile of leaves.
In xvi, Eumaeus reports that the old man has deteriorated even
further since Telemachus' departure; he has given up working on
the farm and has stopped eating. Telemachus' reaction to this news
is not very sympathetic, but he orders a messenger to be sent to
revive the old man.

The situation Odysseus finds at Laertes' farm, then, is precisely
what the rest of the epic would lead us to expect: the fine farm well-
kept, and showing evidence of the old man's hard labor, Laertes
himself pitifully decrepit and a little peculiar, wearing a goatskin
cap which Homer finds particularly noteworthy.

Was Laertes ever king? Homer is indeed hazy on this point in
earlier references, but then again, he is somewhat hazy here, and
in fact, throughout the epic he is vague about the whole idea of
kingship. As Whitman points out,[12] "clearly the title 'king' is
losing its meaning, and is taking on the one familiar in Hesiod,
namely, 'lord of an estate,' or 'nobleman'." [13] Whitman cites i,
383-398, where Telemachus says there are many kings in sea-girt
Ithaca ("βασιλῆες ... πολλοὶ ἐν ἀμφιάλῳ 'Ιθάκῃ") to which Eury-
machus replies that the gods will decide who is to be king in Ithaca
"ὅστις ἐν ἀμφιάλῳ 'Ιθάκῃ βασιλεύσει.") Apparently anyone who
owns land, servants, and a great house is now considered a 'king,'
and his 'kingdom' passes on to his son (i, 387, "ὅ τοι γενεῇ πατρώιόν
ἐστιν."). In Odysseus' case, because only sons are the rule (xvi,
117-120) the succession has been particularly clear: Arkeisios
→ Laertes → Odysseus → Telemachus (see iv, 754-757). This line
of inheritance is not questioned anywhere in the *Odyssey*, although
it is clear that for some reason Odysseus had succeeded his father
long before he left for Troy (he asks Anticleia, in xi, if anyone has
usurped his 'prerogative'—ἐμὸν γέρας—or if Laertes and Telemachus
still hold it? Her reply is that no-one has usurped the καλὸν γέρας;
Telemachus holds the τεμένεα and dines at the magistrates' dinners,
and Laertes stays on the farm).

---

[12] Cedric H. Whitman, *Homer and the Heroic Tradition* (Cambridge,
Mass., 1958), p. 307.

[13] As the editors of Mnemosyne point out, one might add that in Mycenean
qa-si-re-u γωασιλεύς means 'lord, chief' in contrast with wa-na-ka- ωάναξ
'king'. We find many βασιλῆες in the land of the Phaeacians, but only
Alcinoüs ἀνάσσει.

Odysseus' 'kingdom' was apparently in some sense better than any other in Ithaca—he was in some sense a king of kings—but was this because of his personal abilities as a hero and leader, or was it because his estate somehow carried with it the prerogative of leadership in war, or in domestic councils, or were his landholding and palace simply bigger and richer than any other Ithacan 'king's'? Homer does not give us any clear answer to this question.

In xxiv, Laertes is called ποιμὴν λαῶν (i, 368), and he speaks with pride of the time when as 'king' of the Cephallenians (378: "Κεφαλλήνεσσιν ἀνάσσων") he captured Nerikos on the mainland. Neither of these statements calls him βασιλεύς; the latter statement, surely refers to some sort of *pro tempore* war leadership, similar, perhaps to Odysseus' command over the Ithacan contingent at Troy. And why should he not be called a shepherd of men? It is an honorable epithet, fitting for a man who at one time has controlled large landholdings and has governed many serfs. Laertes has never appeared in person before, and this is his big scene; Homer is here increasing the old man's stature (both figuratively and, with divine aid, literally) in preparation for the final episode of the *Odyssey*. Therefore both of Moses Finley's objections seem to me ill-taken; Laertes was—probably—a 'king' before Book xxiv, and he is— probably—a 'king' here; his farm has always been and is now large and well-kept—in short, this scene is in perfect harmony with the rest of the epic.

Dolius and his sons present more of a problem. Why should they appear so late and play such a major part? Where were they when the battle with the suitors was going on? And is Dolius the same Dolius referred to as the father of the despicable Melanthius and Melantho? In the first twenty-three books of the epic there are only four references to a servant named Dolius; iv, 735, xvii, 212, xviii, 322, and xxii, 159. xvii, 212 and xxii, 159 simply name him, as the father of the goatherd Melantheus. xviii, 322 names him as the father of Melantho, who had been raised almost as a daughter by Penelope but repaid her mistress' kindness with insolence and treachery. The first reference to Dolius, however, is in keeping with his appearance in xxiv: Penelope asks Eurycleia to tell her servant Dolius, the old man who tends her orchard, to visit Laertes and bring him up to date on the disappearance of Telemachus. Perhaps, says Penelope, Dolius can persuade the old man to come out of seclusion and approach the townspeople for aid.

It would be idle folly, I think, to argue that Homer had clearly in mind two different characters named Dolius, and that he expected his audience to distinguish between the 'good' one and the 'bad' one on the basis of four brief references in the course of twenty-three books. The only reasonable solution seems to be that *Homerus dormitabat* in this case: in the fourth book he introduced at some length a good servant named Dolius, perhaps vaguely intending to use him as an ally for Odysseus in the battle with the suitors. But thirteen books intervened before the bard returned to the old man; by this time Eumaeus had been introduced as chief servant-ally, and (in Book xvi), Telemachus, in a scene presumably designed to demonstrate to Odysseus that his son had abilities in 'counsel,' had persuaded his father that it would waste too much time to sound out the loyalties of the men on the farms. When Dolius next appears, then, he is named as the father of the 'bad' Melantheus. Perhaps at this point Homer was influenced by the meaning of the name, δόλιος ('treacherous') being an almost too obviously appropriate adjective for the father of the 'black' Melantho and Melantheus.

At any event, when he reached Book xxiv, Homer had another problem. He wanted Odysseus' party to have allies for the big final battle with the suitors' kinsmen. After all, the odds against Odysseus, Telemachus and the two herds in the first battle with the suitors had been mitigated considerably by the surprise situation, their monopoly of arms, and the presence of Athene. The fight with the kinsmen, however, was to be a pitched battle in open country. Would Homer allow his prudent hero to risk an open encounter in which he had little or no chance of winning? It would seem out of character both for Odysseus and for his creator: totally unrealistic battle situations do not appear in the Homeric repertoire.

Odysseus, then, needs allies, and Homer has a choice of either introducing an *entirely* new group of loyal servants, or bringing in the already-mentioned Dolius and as large a number of strong sons as could be credited. Maybe the first choice would have been wiser; certainly, there is something repulsive about the thought of Telemachus sitting down to a jolly lunch with the father and brothers of a man whom he has just horribly massacred and mutilated. But, just as this thought does not occur to most readers of the *Odyssey*, it undoubtedly did not occur to Homer's audience, nor, perhaps, to the bard himself. In any event, the bad taste

4

inherent in the scene is no argument against Homer as author; it would have been equally tactless of a forger. The inconsistency in the character of Dolius is not the work of the twenty-fourth book; it is already present in iv versus xvii, xviii and xxii. And the Dolius we find here in Book xxiv accords very well with the initial portrait in the fourth book; he is an old man, and a friend of Laertes. Even his special relationship to Penelope can be seen in xxiv where he anxiously asks if the wise queen knows of her husband's return. This question, incidentally, seems to suggest a further point: that the author of xxiv was not ignorant of Dolius' role in xvii, xviii, and xxii, for he makes it clear here that the old man and his sons have not heard about the battle in the hall and thus of the deaths of Melantheus and Melantho. The point is not pressed explicitly; that would be pointing out the delicacy of the situation to the presumably oblivious audience, but that the point is even implied seems to me to indicate that the bard knew he had got himself into a ticklish spot, and wanted quietly to reconcile the two sides of Dolius for the sake of any hearers who might have been listening a bit too closely.

Dolius, in short, is carelessly handled—but he is carelessly handled throughout the *Odyssey*. There is no indication that the blunder is not Homer's own, here as before. The old servant and his sons do serve a useful purpose as allies and that, apparently, justified their appearance sufficiently for the bard.

Odysseus' cruelty to his old father is a favorite target of critics. Page, for example, is ecstatic with irony: "It is all very lively and amusing and decadent . . .," [14] he says, "only it pays no respect whatever to the story which it interrupts." Spohn [15] says that in the case of the servants and of Telemachus and Penelope there were good reasons for Odysseus to withhold his identity until he was sure of their loyalty, but here, with his decrepit old father it is simply and gratuitously mean. Well, yes, it is. Few modern students, I imagine, can read this episode for the first time without feeling pity for old Laertes and exasperation with Odysseus—but equally few would deny, I think, that this behavior is utterly characteristic of Odysseus as he has been presented throughout the epic. His homecoming in Book xiii is particularly illuminating:

---

[14] Page, *op. cit.*, p. 112.
[15] Spohn, *op. cit.*

Athene, the hero's divine counterpart in craftiness (as she herself points out in 296-9), teases him in precisely the same way as he teases Laertes in xxiv; he does not know the island is Ithaca, and she withholds the information until the end of a very long speech. (Surely this behavior is equally 'cruel' of Athene—poor Odysseus has been wandering for so many years; why should she gratuitously prolong his sufferings?). He in return replies with a long lying story—true to his nature, as Homer says in 255: "αἰεὶ ἐνὶ στήθεσσι νόον πολυκερδέα νωμῶν"—"always keeping in his breast a crafty mind." She is characteristically delighted with his myth-making and praises him highly for it. More by-play follows, during which he urges the goddess to tell him where he really is, and her answer is significant: this is why I will never desert you, she says, because you are so shrewd and so wary; any ordinary man would rush right home to see his wife, but not you, you have to make sure and have the proof of your senses.

This, then, is the core of Odysseus' character, and it has the approval of a goddess—Odysseus is not the 'ordinary' spontaneous, affectionate man; he lies instinctively and he waits instinctively. His behavior with Laertes is characteristic—if he acted in this one instance like the 'ordinary' man, then indeed we might suspect the authenticity of the episode; as it is, the scene achieves precisely those emotions which Homer is apparently so interested in and so adept at creating; painful suspense, followed by a sudden release of spontaneous feeling. This sort of teasing is also characteristic of Serbo-Croatian oral epic (as are protracted recognition scenes.) In the wedding of Smailagić Meho, for example, the hero tells his father—merely "to test him"—that he did *not* rescue the heroine Fatima, when in fact he did. The old man nearly kills the boy, before the truth comes out. And Homer, like Odysseus, is also fond of teasing by holding back; instances in both epics are numerous, but perhaps the best examples are, in the *Iliad*, the long series of delays which keep Achilles from entering the battle after he has decided to do so, and in the *Odyssey*, the long speech of Polyphemus to the ram under which our hero is literally 'hanging in suspense.'

Now, I think, we are at a good point to progress to the positive defense of the episode. For even if the criticisms of the Laertes scene were doubled or tripled, it would still be difficult for the critics to get around the fact that this scene is *necessary*. The audience has been led to expect a reunion with Laertes. As Scott says,[16] "two matters for which the poet makes careful preparation are still undecided when Odysseus and his wife retire to their chamber: first, will the suitors die unavenged, and secondly, what will Laertes do when he hears of his son's return?" We will take up the first of these questions in the next chapter; for the second, let us quickly detail the preparations Homer has made for a Laertes scene.

Laertes is mentioned by name twenty-one times in the first twenty-three books of the *Odyssey*. The most important of these references are as follows: 1) He is first referred to in the first book. Athene, disguised as Mentes, describes the old man as a pathetic recluse who tires himself out working on his farm. 2) In the second book Antinoos, telling the story of Penelope's web, notes that she was weaving the shroud for Laertes. Penelope argued that she would be reviled by the whole Achaean people if she allowed her father-in-law—who had acquired so much wealth (ii, 102) to be buried without a ceremonial robe, and her argument convinced the suitors. Once again, then, Laertes has been presented as (a) dignified and important but (b) very old. 3) In the fourth book (iv, 111) Menelaus cites Laertes first, before Penelope and Tele-machus, in his list of those who must be grieving for Odysseus. 4) iv, 734-757: Penelope's interview with Eurycleia: Penelope suggests that Dolius should ask Laertes to come to town and plead with the people. This is worth noting—it shows that Penelope at least still considers the old man capable of stirring himself to some effort, and it shows that presumably an appeal from him would be expected to carry weight with the townspeople. Eurycleia replies that the old man has troubles enough, and that the blessed gods will always keep the Arkeisian line in possession of their grand house and fertile lands. So here, too, both Laertes' pathetic old age and his important position have been stressed. 5) In the under-world, Odysseus questions his mother first about her death, second about Laertes, third about Telemachus, fourth about Penelope. As is consistent with Homeric chiastic style, Anticleia's replies are in reverse order: Penelope has not remarried and is still at home; Telemachus still holds the τεμένεα and dines with magistrates; Laertes is in a sorry state, wearing rags and sleeping on leaves,

---

[16] Scott, "The Close of the *Odyssey*," p. 401.

because of his longing for you; I died of the same longing. 6) xiv, 171-3: here again Laertes is listed (this time by Eumaeus) as one of the three who long for Odysseus. 7) xv, 353-7: Eumaeus describes Laertes as continually praying for death, so grieved is he by the absence of Odysseus and the death of Anticleia. 8) xvi, 137-153: Eumaeus suggests to Telemachus that it would be kind to inform not just Penelope, but also Laertes of his safe return. For, he says, even in his grief for Odysseus the old man was able to work and eat, but upon Telemachus' disappearance he stopped working altogether and is starving himself to death. So once again we have the familiar family triad: Penelope, Telemachus, Laertes. These three are The Family; these are the three who mourn Odysseus' absence; these are the people who matter in Ithaca.

Each one of these eight passages leads the audience to expect an eventual reunion between Odysseus and Laertes, and their cumulative effect is such that if the *Odyssey* ended at xxiii, 296, surely the first question which would occur, to school children as well as to scholars, would be "What happened to Laertes?" Some sort of Laertes scene is clearly called for by the whole pattern of the epic. Thus the critic, if he wishes to reject *this* Laertes scene, must adopt one of the historical hypotheses suggested in the Appendix (e.g. Homer died and left the work unfinished; there was originally a different Laertes scene for which this one has been substituted, etc.) This process undoubtedly has some appeal for those who are already emotionally committed to rejecting the Laertes episode as given in our mss., but it seems cumbersome and unnecessary. For not only is a Laertes scene called for by the epic, but *this* Laertes scene—handled as it is handled here—seems to me to be characteristic of Homer at nearly the top of his form. If this latter statement is correct, as I will try to show, then anti-Homeric hypotheses become more and more tenuous and difficult to generate, for they must explain not only how a forgery came to take place but also how that forgery came to be of Homeric calibre. In sum, the naive assumption that Homer wrote this scene as well as the rest of the *Odyssey* would then become the simplest hypothesis to fit the simple data.

Why is this scene, in my estimation, characteristic of Homer at —almost—his best? A few secondary reasons have already been given: Odysseus' behavior is entirely in character, Laertes is precisely as we have been led to expect, the suspense in the initial interview is skillfully handled to produce a maximum of anxiety and pity in the audience, and the hearer's happy relief at the ultimate revelation is correspondingly great—the scene is, in short, carefully contrived for emotional power. But even more important are the passages in which Odysseus proves his identity. This is the last recognition scene in the epic, and is, one might say, the loveliest, even superior to the reunion with Penelope.

Whitman has given the whole series of recognitions a thorough and fascinating analysis:[17] "The modes of revelation tell more than the identity of the stranger; they rehearse his roles as father, hero, king, husband, and son. Telemachus, though he could have had no recollection of his father, had often imagined him ... when he hears that it is Odysseus, he believes, with youth's credulity, instantly without token or proof ... Argus the dog is just the opposite; to him there is not even a disguise, it is simply Odysseus ... Then come the recognitions by the scar. This is a token which would mean nothing to Telemachus, but everything to Eurycleia, Eumaeus, and Philoetius, since they were present when Odysseus got the scar, and it is to them the emblem of the true king. ... To the suitors, there can be only one appropriate form of revelation —the bow ... So at the end of Book xxii the father, the true master, the touchstone of the moral order, and the hero have all revealed themselves. There remain the husband, and the son, or heir .... Husband and wife have secret signs, which others do not know, says Penelope; and somewhat like a new bride, she cannot speak or look at Odysseus. Then comes the recognition of the marriage bed ... and she will have only the man who knows the nature of that steadfast bed and, therewith, her own nature." And in the scene with Laertes, Whitman concludes, Odysseus "names the trees which his father gave him as a child, thus in a way declaring his patrimony, his knowledge of the land, and his right to it. He recreates, by continuity with the past and with the land, his role as the rightful and legitimate heir. And with this recognition Odysseus has, in a sense, restored his selfhood completely."

Is Whitman just reading things into the simple text? Are not these recognitions by token, like the footprints and locks of hair in Attic drama and the strawberry-marks of costume melodrama,

---

[17] Whitman, *op. cit.*, pp. 301-305.

just a popular entertainment device, a rather easy trick for pleasing audiences who are amused by that sort of thing? Perhaps so—but if so, we might ask why audiences *do* so persistently like that sort of thing; why are popular folk-tale plots popular; why do certain motifs and gimmicks and devices keep recurring and pleasing crowds? Is it not that they can be felt in some way to be getting at something important and true about life? And what could recognitions by token be getting at?—The always interesting question of what the Self is; what *I* am. How am I different from all those millions of other people around me? Is there a Real Me, distinct from that brave face I put on that most of the world thinks is Me? Is there a Me that stays the same even when my body ages and suffers accident, even when my opinions change and my manners are altered by time?

The best recognition scenes of Homer offer—symbolically and perhaps unconsciously—an answer to this naive but certainly perplexing question: the Real Me is my past, my memory (shared or not shared with others) of my unique and continuous experience in the world. Thus to Penelope the Real Odysseus is her young husband who built their marriage bed with a root in the earth.

The Laertes recognition is even nicer: to Laertes (and to Odysseus vis-à-vis Laertes) the real Odysseus is the little boy trotting after his father in the orchard. Can it be pure accident that trees are central to the two major recognition scenes of the *Odyssey*? A great olive is the rooted foundation of Odysseus' and Penelope's marriage bed; thus wisdom—it is Athene's own tree—and the endurance of the earth go to make up their marriage. And what does the hero receive from and share with this father? Pear trees, apples, figs, and vines; fruit-bearing trees. Odysseus' relationship with his father, like his marriage, is a bond founded on nature, but the emphasis here is less on constancy and more on growth and fruitfulness: "Each vine ripened at a different time," recalls the hero, (342-4) "so that the bunches of grapes were at different stages when the season of Zeus above loaded the branches." So too father and son and grandson are at different stages. Laertes has had his season of ripeness; Odysseus is now mature, but he in turn will be succeeded by Telemachus; fruitfulness and change go together, and the father must in time give over to his son. It is not merely a question of rightful ownership of the land (although Odysseus establishes that, too, in this speech); the gift which a father gives his son is life, and the right to give life in turn to *his* son. And memory makes the process a continuous one.

This shared memory of having once been father and son, giver and recipient, landowner and heir, is what makes Laertes and Odysseus father and son now, when both are altered physically almost beyond recognition. It is a pleasing picture, and a touching one. If Odysseus had merely shown his father the scar, which would have been all the plot required, the revelation would have been crushingly anti-climactic after the Penelope recognition—but as we have it here, it is the crowning episode of the series.[18]

---

[18] Erbse thinks the Laertes scene so simple, natural and appropriate that he considers it to be the "original", on which the other recognition scenes of the poem were based. He says (p. 109) "It is not conceivable that these simpler forms could have resulted from the imitation of previous, more complicated ones . . . at least this portion of Book xxiv was contained in his (Homer's) poetic purpose from the very beginning". (translated by Sharon Jackiw.) Fenik, *Studies*, 47-50, on the other hand, finds the scene *un*natural and *in*appropriate, but he does not commit himself on its authenticity; the inappropriateness, he says, is of a sort which appears throughout the *Odyssey*.

VII. THE FINAL FIGHT

Swiftly through the town runs Rumor the Messenger, telling of
the suitors' terrible death and fate. A crowd soon gathers at the
palace of Odysseus; the bodies of the foreign suitors are dispatched
to their several homelands, and the Ithacan corpses are buried by
their kinsmen. The Ithacans then gather in assembly. Against the
advice of Medon the herald and Halitherses the seer, the majority
of the Ithacans rally around Eupeithes the father of Antinoos, and
prepare to meet Odysseus in battle. A brief interlude on Olympus
follows, in which Zeus encourages Athene to make peace, and suggests that the gods should overlook Odysseus' blood-guilt. The
party of Odysseus goes to meet the enemy; Laertes, with Athene's
help, kills Eupeithes. The Ithacans are put to flight, and Odysseus
and his allies are in hot pursuit when they are stopped by a thunder-
bolt from Zeus. Athene, in the guise of Mentor, concludes the
treaty of peace, establishing Odysseus in his kingdom at last.

The objections to this final episode all, so far as I know, fall into
one category only: aesthetic objections. But the critics make up in
vehemence for what they lack in concrete evidence: "In extremo
deinde libro," says J. G. Schneider,[1] "auctorem ingenium et
spiritus plane defecisse videtur: ita, ut in rerum multarum satis
gravium narratione brevitate inepta, partim etiam obscura de-
functus, lectoris exspectationem plane fallat." Spohn, who quotes
this statement, particularly objects to the brief Olympian council,
which he thinks hasty and badly written; Page concurs in this
opinion, and adds,[2] "From this moment onwards the story rushes
spasmodically and deviously to its lame conclusion." "It may be
judged," writes Kirk, "a suitably weak or inept conclusion to a
final episode, that is ludicrous in its staccato leaps hither and thither,
its indigestible concoction of rustics, thunderbolts, feeble old men
and a goddess disguised or undisguised." [3] The last episode of the
Odyssey, then, is said to be lame, hasty, awkward, abrupt.

I must admit that I agree. This last scene is the one part of the

---

[1] *Praef, Orph. Argonaut.* (1806), pp. 34 ff., cited in Spohn.
[2] Page, *Homeric Odyssey*, p. 113.
[3] Kirk, *Songs*, p. 250.

Conclusion which seems to me to bring Homer's name scant credit,
the one scene which I would like to imagine the dying poet entrust-
ing to his dutiful but prosaic son, with instructions about necessary
contents, but none, alas, about style. But my wish and my value
judgment have no bearing on whether or not the scene is genuine.
In the 20th century, in English, we place greatest emphasis on the
last words of a sentence, a paragraph, a poem, a long work; clearly,
this was not the taste of the ancient Greek. The great *Oedipus* ends
in a way which seems to us weak, anticlimactic, disappointing, but
it is unquestionably the work of Sophocles. The ending of the
Iliad, too, is rather weary and mechanical: appropriately so, for
the funeral of Hector marks the end of the Trojans' hope. In the
Odyssey, the tone of exhaustion, of getting the whole thing over
with, is less appropriate. But the ancient audience, not expecting
a grand finale, may not have minded in the least. And even if
they did mind, if the ending is poor even by ancient standards,
we still cannot know that Homer did not write it. It is a necessary
scene; that we *do* know.

What features do we find in this last episode which make it seem
necessary or particularly fitting for the last scene of the *Odyssey*?
First, the Olympian Council, which Page and Spohn find offensive
and unnecessary, is important both to give dignity and importance
to the closing scene—as Pope saw—and to free Odysseus and Ithaca
officially from the miasma of blood guilt. The latter feature of the
scene is particularly important; Odysseus had committed murder
—if justly—and some sort of purification was clearly called for if
no act of vengeance was to take place. How could such an issue be
settled except by divine fiat? Carpenter, Lang, and Wolf concur
about this function of the Olympian conference and of Athene's
interference at the end. "Except by a *Dea ex machina*," says Lang,[4]
"this feud, according to heroic manners, could in no wise be reconciled." We would leave the performance still fearing for Odysseus, says Wolf,[5] "nisi amnestia et pax fieret deorum interventu
et subita μηχανῇ." And the *dea ex machina* ending, suggests Carpenter,[6] "may have appealed as much to a Homeric as to a later
Euripidean audience, being a proper Greek way to end a heroic
narrative of violence."

---

[4] Lang, *Homer and the Epic*, p. 318.
[5] *Proleg.*, p. 136, cited by Spohn, *op. cit.*
[6] Carpenter, *Folk Tale*, etc., p. 193.

So much for the alleged 'unnecessary' interference of the gods. That the human part of the episode, the battle, is a necessity, and that the audience has been led to expect such a scene, is even more clear, and has been noted by Dacier, Pope, Merry, and Scott, among others.[7]

There are four "plants" which prepare the audience for an eventual reconciliation with the suitors' kinsmen. In Book i, 378-80, Telemachus says to the suitors, "I shall pray to the gods who are forever that Zeus at last grant me vengeance, and that you may perish in this house unavenged (νήποινοι)." In Book ii (143-5), he repeats this statement in front of the Ithacan assembly, and Zeus confirms his prayer with an auspicious display of two eagles. The third reference is more explicit: In the beginning of Book xx, Odysseus confides to Athene that he is worried about the coming conflict with the suitors. "But there is another and *greater* problem on my mind," he adds. (xx, 41-3). "If, with your help and that of Zeus, I kill them, where can I flee for safety?" In the fourth scene, xxiii, 111-140, Odysseus puts the problem squarely to Telemachus: "When a man has killed just one person in his town," he says, "even if the victim has few friends to avenge him, the murderer flees, leaving his family and native land. But *we* have destroyed the very cornerstone of the city—the pick of Ithaca's youth." Telemachus offers encouragement but no suggestions, and Odysseus conceives the plan of pretending the palace is holding a wedding-feast, so that he and his party can slip away to the farm, to await further developments, and presumably to gather allies.

This last scene, so unmistakably a plant for the two final episodes of the epic, has caused the critics to perform some understandable juggling. Allen's solution is that "the carrying out of what is admitted necessary is left to the reader's imagination." [8] By showing that Odysseus *planned* a reconciliation with the suitors' kinsmen, Homer, according to Allen, "innocently" thought he had satisfied the requirements of the plot. But is this sort of "innocence" characteristic of Homer? Does he anywhere else 'solve' so important a dilemma (after stating that dilemma in the strongest possible terms) simply by saying that the hero recognized the problem and

---

[7] Dacier, p. 287 f., cited by Spohn; Alexander Pope, *The Odyssey of Homer*, trans. with notes (London, 1806), vol. 6, p. 120; Merry, *Odyssey*, p. xv; Scott, "The Close of the *Odyssey*,", p. 401.

[8] Allen, *Origins*, p. 219.

intended to cope with it? Does the *Iliad* end with Achilles' decision
to kill Hector, leaving the actual carrying out of that decision to
the reader's imagination? Is the Cyclops plot resolved as soon as
Odysseus admits that the situation is a difficult one which will
require some clever planning? Allen's reasoning here is on a par
with Ko-Ko's in the *Mikado*: "When your Majesty says, 'Let a
thing be done,' it's as good as done—practically, it *is* done—because
your Majesty's will is law. Your Majesty says, 'kill a gentleman,'
and a gentleman is told off to be killed. Consequently, that gentleman is as good as dead—practically he *is* dead—and if he is dead,
why not say so?"

Page does not fall into this sort of absurdity; his solution is the
time-honored one of declaring the opposing evidence invalid.
Since the xxiii episode clearly prepares for the last scenes of xxiv,
the xxiii scene must itself be athetized. "There is no more ruinous
interpolation in the *Odyssey* than this," he pronounces.[9] He is not
very convincing about just *why* it is so ruinous—the episode interrupts the Penelope-Odysseus recognition, but surely Page is not
so unfamiliar with Homer as not to realize that both the *Iliad* and
the *Odyssey* are made up of innumerable such delays and inter-
ruptions of the main course of the plot; would he athetize every
banquet, every sacrifice, every bath, and every long simile which
stays the forward progress of the action in either epic? No, the
'ruinousness' of this passage seems chiefly to consist in its clear
connection with the Laertes and Battle episodes.

Page is indulging in the risky practice of cutting off the legs of a
table, for if he lops off this scene, because he wants to lop off the
last scene, he must also athetize xxiii, 297-9, which refers to the
dancing for which Odysseus plans in this scene. But if he throws
out 297-9, then he is not at liberty to choose any ending in xxiii
later than 296, which, as we noted in Chapter Two, would conclude
the epic with an uncompleted μὲν. Then, too, there are the references
in i and ii to the suitors' remaining νήποινοι; to make his table
balance really well, Page should also find these passages ruinous.
And more important, he clearly must find something wrong with
the Book xx passage, for in it Odysseus says that the problem of
what to do after killing the suitors is an even greater problem than
the suitors themselves. It is *possible*, of course, that all of these

---

[9] Page, *op. cit.*, p. 115.

atheteses would be justified, that our clever (but inept) rhapsode did go through the entire *Odyssey* inserting references to Laertes and the problem of reconciliation, just to prepare his audience for the new ending he was planning to tack on to the epic—but we have absolutely no evidence for this. Thus we may, I think, suspect that Page, in excising this one inconvenient bit of evidence, has merely scotched the snake, not killed it.

The battle episode, then, seems to be necessary both because of the internal preparations made for it in the *Odyssey* and externally because of the demands of the ancient blood feud. The story of Odysseus is not complete until he is at peace with the citizens of Ithaca; as Mme. Dacier remarks, "Le sujet du Poëme de L'Odyssée n'est pas seulement le retour d'Ulysse dans sa maison, mais le retour d'Ulysse rétabli dans son Palais, reconnu de toute sa famille, et en paisible possession de ses États." [10]

Outside of providing the final resolution to these problems, does the closing scene serve any other Homeric purposes? Three according to my count. The first, as pointed out by Scott and others, is that it provides a final bow for Athene and thus gives the whole epic a nice chiastic balance; "the poem is set in motion by Athena, it is brought to an end by the same goddess," [11] as Scott says. The second requires a little more speculation on our part: the epic ends with Mentor (the disguised Athene). Pope's explanation of the passage is interesting:[12] He suggests that the appearance of Athene-Mentor really means, "when stript of its poetical ornaments," that Mentor, as a wise man, acted as mediator between the two opposing parties—"this being an act of wisdom, poetry ascribes it to Minerva." Mentor is then a real man, and is here taking his final bow.

But even if we reject this ingenious interpretation and regard Mentor as no more than a convenient disguise adopted by the goddess, we must acknowledge that her choice of disguise is singularly appropriate for the concluding action of the epic: as the *Odyssey* is in great part a story about learning, about education, and as the *Telemachia* is the most clearly educational part of that story, so it is fitting for the whole to be concluded by Athene in her guise as the patroness of Telemachus. It is not Athene the personal friend of Odysseus, nor Athene the champion of justice

[10] Dacier, *loc. cit.*
[11] Scott, *Unity*, p. 263.
[12] Pope, *op. cit.*, p. 164.

who performs the final pacification, it is Athene the Teacher, the guide of the inexperienced.[13]

The third purpose served by the battle episode is to show the three generations, Laertes, Odysseus, and Telemachus, fighting side by side. As we have seen before, the family is a central concern of the whole epic. As opposed to the *Iliad*, the *Odyssey* is overwhelmingly domestic in orientation; Homer has throughout the poem taken great care not only to point out the importance of having a good family but also to provide numerous characters who serve as parallels or contrasts for his basic family group of Laertes-Odysseus-Penelope-Telemachus.

Let us take Penelope first. She plays two principal roles in the *Odyssey*, the Faithful Wife and the Wise Woman. In the first role, she is domestic, dutiful, chaste, human, and slightly uninteresting. Homer has provided two explicit contrasts for her in this role, Clytaemnestra, whose disloyalty is contrasted with Penelope's fidelity, and Calypso, whose divinity is contrasted with Penelope's ordinary humanness. The symbol of her wifely relationship to Odysseus is the marriage bed of the recognition scene, steadfast and rooted in the earth.

As a Wise Woman, Penelope becomes a far more interesting character, for it is in this role that Homer makes her the feminine counterpart of Odysseus himself. She is clever like Odysseus (as in the web trick), and skilled in common τέχνη like Odysseus (see ii, 116-18, where Antinoos explicitly attributes both her intelligence and her skill in handicraft to Odysseus' patroness Athene), but above all, she has her husband's almost exasperating cautiousness (see xxiii, 166-70, where Odysseus berates her 'abnormal' holding-back in a speech strikingly similar to Athene's in xiii, where the goddess points out his own unnaturalness in not rushing home to see his wife immediately). But Penelope's wisdom is, of course, woman's wisdom, and therefore not precisely the same as Odysseus' male variety—she learns the truth in dreams, from omens, or Athene prompts her to do precisely the right thing; as Anne Amory says, "Odysseus knows what he knows, but Penelope's knowledge is often unconscious. . . . (but) her intuitive penetration is both profound and accurate." [14]

---

[13] Although Clarke (*The Art of the Odyssey*, pp. 84-5) thinks Athene here represents Justice, one of the two major themes (with Love) of the poem.
[14] Amory, *op. cit.*, p. 173.

Does the *Odyssey* give us any character parallels for Penelope in her role as wise woman? Arete is one, but surprisingly enough, the outstanding example is Helen. One might expect Helen, as almost the archetypal unfaithful wife to be provided as a contrast for Penelope, but Homer has chosen to underplay this aspect of Helen's character and to emphasize instead her intelligence. Like Penelope's, Helen's wisdom is intuitive—she interprets omens and she recognizes Telemachus instantly—but she is more of a witch than Penelope, and more divine. This divinity of Helen's, in fact is to be responsible for Menelaus' translation to the Elysian fields after death—thus, interestingly enough, it is his wife who will be the cause of his ultimate blessedness, just as it was Agamemnon's wife who was responsible for his ultimate misery—and as Odysseus' wife was a cause (if not the sole cause) of his final felicity.

The father-son relationship is equally important. We have already seen (in Chapter Five) that Homer explicitly compares Odysseus-Telemachus with Agamemnon-Orestes, and with Achilles-Neoptolemus. Another significant comparison is with Nestor-Peisistratus, and Nestor-Antilochus, but more significant, perhaps, is the brief reference to Menelaus' natural son Megapenthes, whose wedding to a Spartan girl is being celebrated jointly with Hermione's wedding to Neoptolemus in the beginning of Book iv. This is not an important reference, of course, but it shows, I think, how much concerned Homer was with exalting the father-son relationship. Tradition had, apparently, already established that Helen bore no sons; therefore the bard, in order to show Menelaus as a happy man, goes to the trouble of exalting a slave's child to the status of a son whose wedding would be celebrated on an equal level with that of Helen's legitimate daughter.

The central question of the *Telemacheia* is posed first by Athene in i (206-7): "Is Telemachus really the son of Odysseus?" Telemachus' reply to this apparently innocent and literal question is "my mother says I am. But I do not know." Surely this is more than just a question of the boy's legitimacy; in the second book, Athene takes up the theme again, praising Telemachus for his conduct in the Assembly and suggesting that he has inherited Odysseus' talent for debate. But she observes, few sons are as good as their fathers (ii, 276), and this is the problem: Telemachus is clearly the son of Odysseus biologically, and he looks like him (as Athene and Helen both point out), but is he really the man his father was and is? Telemachus has faults in the beginning of the book, but they are chiefly faults of youth and inexperience; he lacks 'spirit,' which Athene puts into him; he lacks faith in the power of the gods (for which the goddess scolds him roundly, iii, 230-1) and he lacks courtly manners (ii, 22-4), which he learns in the course of his grand tour.

But the real test of Telemachus as a man does not come until Book xxi: three times he tries to bend his father's bow, and the fourth he is about to succeed when Odysseus, with a gesture, warns him not to. The symbolism is, I think, clear: Telemachus is *almost* the man his father is. It would be somehow disappointing if the son were found to be in every respect the equal of his father, but this is a satisfying approximation: Telemachus is a slightly tamer version of his father (and at the same time, more bloodthirsty: it is he who mutilates Melantheus and hangs the maids, while it is Odysseus who rebukes Eurycleia for exulting over the dead), but he is his 'true son' and contributes largely to Odysseus' final blessedness.

With all this emphasis on fathers and sons—and with the poem's emphasis on heredity in general (e.g. even Eurycleia and Eumaeus are revealed as having been borne of noble parents), it would be surprising indeed if Laertes, too, were not given his share of hero-ism. For the first twenty-three books of the epic, his role, necessa-rily, was that of the pitiful old man, but it was made clear that his decline was premature and self-willed, the result chiefly of his beloved son's disappearance. That he should have a moment of glory in battle—made plausible by Athene's aid and the probable weakness of his target, another old man—is far more satisfying and wonderful (and far better suited to the tastes of the heroic age) than that he should applaud his son's heroism feebly from the sidelines. This is the real crown of Odysseus' triumph, that his son, emboldened to heroism by his presence, and his father, re-juvenated by his return, should both fight at his side against strong odds in a virtuous and victorious cause.

Before the battle Odysseus urges Telemachus to prove himself worthy of the family reputation; "Your line will not be shamed by me," replies Telemachus, to which Laertes adds, "Dear gods, what a day this is for me to rejoice in; my son and my grandson are competing in honor!" It is at this point that Athene addresses Laertes by his patronymic, "son of Arkeisios," and his great moment has come. This scene is the ideal vindication of Odysseus' domestic style of life, and here is the ultimate triumph of the family.

VIII. CONCLUSIONS

"Those oft are strategems which error seem,
Nor is it Homer nods, but we that dream."
—Pope, *Essay on Criticism*

We have come, like Odysseus, to the end of our trials. Now let us, in the manner of our hero, epitomize those long and devious wanderings, and see what we have learned.

In Chapter One, several hypotheses were suggested for the historical origin of xxiv. The first group attempted to explain how xxiv could seem so fitting if its author were not Homer; the second group, which assumed that Homer *was* its author, suggested possible origins of the difficulties in xxiv. We then asserted the ambitious hope that this dissertation would persuade its readers to prefer one of the latter group of hypotheses.

After a brief chapter on oral theory, chapter three dealt with the Penelope episode. We digressed briefly on the Alexandrian condemnation of xxiii, 296-xxiv, 548, and rather tentatively accepted the unitarian theory that by τέλος Aristarchus meant "goal" and not "conclusion." Arguing that Aristarchus' disapproval of the conclusion was not in any case to be relied on excessively, we pointed out that he gave no documentary evidence for his opinion, and that the Alexandrians often based their atheteses on what are now considered fallacious critical standards.

Next we considered the problem of possible endingplaces for the *Odyssey*. If the epic were not to conclude at xxiv, 548, we found that only four other stopping points were possible: xxiii, 296, which would conclude the epic with an unanswered μὲν, and xxiii, 299, 309, and 343, which do not have even the dubious authority of the Alexandrians in their favor. All four, we noted, would end the *Odyssey* on a private note, which we felt, would seem odd in Homer.

Odysseus' epitome of his adventures was then discussed and found to be a characteristic Homeric device, for which there are striking parallels in the *Iliad*. Further, we noted that if we accept the whole Conclusion, then each part of the *Odyssey's* three-fold plot is epitomized at some point in the epic: the Telemacheia in Book xvii, the Sea Tales in xxiii, the Revenge in xxiv.

Chapters Four and Five considered the Nekuia. The standard Aristarchan criticisms about hell's geography were dismissed as trivial. We then considered the novelty of Hermes Psychopompos, who suited the bard in six ways: 1) a god adds importance and solemnity to any critical scene; 2) important deaths in the *Iliad* are always treated in an unusual manner; 3) a guide is dramatically necessary to initiate action on the suitors' part; 4) Hermes plays a similar role in the last book of the *Iliad*; 5) Hermes has chthonic connections in both epics; and 6) Hermes bears a special relationship to Odysseus; he and Athene share between them the two halves of the hero's wisdom—and this is the god's final bow in the epic. On the burial question, we decided that there, too, close examination of evidence from the *Iliad* shows no consistent Homeric position. Only one scene (Patroclus' ghost speech) implies that an unburied shade cannot enter the underworld; other scenes, in both epics, strongly imply the contrary.

In Chapter Five we took up the problem of Amphimedon's epitome of the Revenge plot. His story of the web was found to be chronologically consistent with the rest of the *Odyssey*. As for his blunder about Penelope's part in the revenge plot, we concluded that whatever the poet's reason for letting Amphimedon err about this, the amount of detailed information that the ghost gets correct clearly indicates that his speech was composed for our *Odyssey* and not for any other version of the tale.

Finally, we pointed out five reasons why the Nekuia cannot be called an unnecessary or irrelevant episode: 1) it provides the third epitome; 2) it provides Penelope with almost the only praise she receives for her twenty years of fidelity; 3) it provides an impressive description of a funeral; 4) it provides a last bow for several major characters of the *Iliad* and *Odyssey*; 5) it provides a final comparison and contrast of the characters of Agamemnon and Achilles with Odysseus.

The Laertes episode was the subject of the sixth chapter. After a brief digression on philological problems, we demonstrated that the picture given of Laertes in this scene is entirely consistent with the rest of the epic. The problem of the servant Dolius, we found, was a problem of earlier books of the *Odyssey*—in which he was inconsistently presented—and not a problem of this episode, in which he serves the useful function of ally for the coming battle. We pointed out that the rest of the epic clearly prepares the audience for a reunion with Laertes, and that the episode is not only suspenseful, quite in the manner of Homer, but also provides the climactic recognition scene of a masterful and meaningful series.

In Chapter Seven, we discussed the aesthetic objections to the Battle scene, and dismissed them as irrelevant. The scene, we found, is necessary both because it has been "planted" for several times previously in the epic, and because of the Greek attitude toward bloodguilt and the necessity for revenge. Also, we concluded, the scene provides an appropriate final bow for Athene, who initiated the action of the epic, and for Mentor (Athene) as the patron of education. Finally, the scene, with father, son, and grandson fighting side by side, provides the most appropriate possible ending for a tale concerned primarily with the family.

Of the four scenes in xxiii, 296-xxiv, 548, then, two—the third and the fourth—are necessary to the plot of the *Odyssey*, and seem from the evidence of the earlier books of the epic to have been part of the author's original design. And if we accept these two episodes, there is no reason not to accept the first (Penelope) episode as well. This would leave only the Nekuia in doubt—the episode whose only serious fault, it would seem, is that, since Homer did not lead his audience to expect such a scene and it comes as a surprise, it could be dispensed with.

The *Odyssey* is a story with a plot. That plot, the return of Odysseus to Ithaca, his revenge on the suitors, and his re-establishment in his family and kingdom, is only completed with the *spondai* effected by Athene in the last episode. But the *Odyssey* is more than a story with a plot; it is also, I believe, a story with a theme, and to this theme all four scenes of the Conclusion—and *especially* the 'unnecessary' Nekuia—are vital. What is that theme?—That the Wise Man is a greater hero than the simple Soldier, the World is a better proving-ground than the Battle-field, and the Home superior to the Camp. The *Odyssey* criticises, I think, the limited value-system of the typical heroes of the *Iliad*, of Ajax, of Diomedes, and especially of Achilles, and glorifies in their place the more nearly all-embracing values of the flexible Odysseus.

In the end, the mighty Agamemnon is only Agamemnon the cuckold and victim, and even the divine Achilles is only Achilles the dead soldier. But Odysseus is Odysseus the traveller, Odysseus the bard, Odysseus the hero, Odysseus the husband, the father, the son, and finally, Odysseus the just king. Of all the heroes of

Troy, only Nestor—the wise man and father—and Menelaus—the husband and traveller—have similar good fortune in this epic.

The theme is two-fold: the hero's wisdom and his domesticity share equal credit for his ultimate success. And both find their final expression in the Conclusion of the epic. Odysseus' epitome of the sea-tales sums up that educative part of the story; the Nekuia makes the final contrast between Odysseus and Agamemnon (in which the decisive factor is not wisdom but the family) and between Odysseus and Achilles (in which Odysseus' flexible style of life, which is equivalent to his 'wisdom,' is found superior to Achilles' simple valor), and the Laertes scene and the final battle conclude the glorification of the family, with Mentor-Athene ("Wisdom") having the last word.

Without the summing-up and clarification provided by these last scenes, the *Odyssey's* theme might have been lost in the course of the epic's intricate and absorbing three-fold plot. With these scenes, the theme is admirably lucid; the conclusion of the epic is therefore both characteristic of the poet of the rest of the Odyssey, and entirely worthy to continue bearing the great name of Homer.

APPENDIX

On page 4 of my introduction, I anticipated that some readers might not be entirely satisfied by my defense of the ending of the *Odyssey*. Some readers might, I thought, perhaps be convinced, by my efforts or their own good reasoning, that the Conclusion *is* necessary and appropriate to the poem, but still be left with a number of still-unsolved problems, a residue of strange words, inexplicable irrelevancies or inconsistencies, and lapses from Homeric greatness. For the sake of these doubters, it is appropriate here to list several plausible historical hypotheses which would account for such a state of affairs. I must say in advance, though, that I do not myself find any of the first four hypotheses either probable or appealing. My readers may judge for themselves. (I'm sure they're relieved to be given this option!).

Hypotheses which account for the peculiar aptness of xxiii, 297-xxiv, 548, but assume that the author of the Odyssey did NOT compose this section:

1. The *Odyssey* originally ended with xxiii, 296. Perhaps, as Mackail thinks,[1] its author died and left it unfinished; perhaps he simply forgot to bind off all the loose ends. Subsequently, an intelligent rhapsode, sensing the incompleteness which we noticed if the work ends at 296, composed the conclusion we now possess.

This is Bury's thesis, except that he postulates as the continuer a disciple of Homer's who "knew the poems thoroughly and was versed in the master's technique," and to whom the dying bard had entrusted the job of completing his own plans for the conclusion.[2] This would not be a historically unparalleled event, but the theory brings Bury so close to the pro-Homer position that one wonders why he did not simply accept the more natural (and parsimonious) idea that "the master" himself composed the conclusion. Bury's postulated near-perfect disciple would explain very few difficulties, so why is it necessary to postulate him at all?

---

[1] J. W. Mackail, "The Epilogue of the Odyssey", in: *Greek Poetry and Life: Essays Presented to Gilbert Murray* (Oxford, 1936), p. 11.
[2] J. B. Bury, "The End of the *Odyssey*", *JHS* 42 (1922), p. 8.

2. The *Odyssey* originally had an ending in which Laertes appeared, the suitors' kinsmen were dealt with, and so on, but this "Homeric" ending was accidentally lost or destroyed in its only manuscript, and our xxiv was written by a rhapsode not out of any devious desire to forge Homer, but simply to provide an appropriate conclusion to the incomplete poem he wished to perform.

3. The *Odyssey* originally had a "Homeric" ending (as in # 2), but some rascally rhapsode substituted our xxiv, to introduce the next epic he was planning to perform—or just to show how clever a Homerid he was. (This, which seems the most far-fetched of the anti-Homer hypotheses, has been adopted by a surprising number of scholars. It remains difficult to imagine any sort of epic for which our xxiv would be a good, or even a possible introduction. An epic about the servant Dolius? About the further adventures of the suitors in the Underworld?)

4. Our extant conclusion is in some parts genuine, but most of it was interpolated later. This hypothesis would allow us to keep what seems absolutely necessary and reject whatever offends. One difficulty, however, is that even among separatists there is very little agreement as to what is necessary and what offensive. The part one would probably reject as least necessary and most puzzling archaeologically would be the second Nekuia. On the other hand, the Laertes scene, while necessary, is the most suspect linguistically. Then again, the very end is the least pleasing aesthetically. (It does seem to weaken the assailant's case, that he is forced to keep switching the grounds for his attack in order to reject every part of the conclusion. Page even goes so far as to reject the end of Book xxiii just because *ipse Aristarchus dixit*, although he finds no fault in it at all.) [3] If we believe Hypothesis # 4 to be correct, then we must also formulate hypotheses to explain why *each* unhomeric part was added or substituted.

Hypotheses which account for difficulties in the conclusion, but assume that the author of the Odyssey composed the ending:

5. Homer (the author of the rest of the *Odyssey*) did compose xxiii, 297 to end, but made liberal use of earlier or alien sources, perhaps to the extent of word-for-word copying, if there were other written texts available in his time. This would explain the

---

[3] Page, *The Homeric Odyssey*, p. 116.

foreignness or inappropriateness of some of his material, but according to the ethics of ancient poetry-making (and modern oral theory) would still make Homer the "author" of our Conclusion. Bowra has suggested that this sort of borrowing may be the source of the Catalogue of Ships. [4]) Too, he might have been borrowing from himself—the description of Achilles' funeral, for example, has something of the set-piece about it, and we can imagine that the bard of the *Odyssey* had probably sung it before, perhaps in a more appropriate but also "Homeric" context.

7. Homer was getting tired and impatient by the time he reached the end of the epic, and allowed himself to make more slips than usual. This obviously makes sense for a dictating oral poet, but is equally possible for a literate author. For example, in *The Picture of Dorian Gray*: the falling-off of attention and effort of the author, after the brilliant first chapter, is so apparent that the work seems to have been written by two different people. Oscar Wilde, clearly, had less stamina than Homer.

8. Homer was getting old by the time he reached the end of the epic: the conclusion was actually written or revised by him at a later date than the beginning of the work, hence new words had come into fashion, the author had been influenced by other poets, and so forth.

But the historical possibilities are manifold; it would seem foolish to commit oneself too strongly to any one in particular. My hope is that this study has whittled the supposed and real difficulties in the Conclusion down to a manageable number, one small enough to permit the reader to favor one of the latter four ("pro-Homer") hypotheses. With regard to the positive, "literary" evidence, I hope I have done more. Someone once said of the Mozart Requiem, "If Mozart didn't write it, than the man who wrote it was a Mozart." I hope that I have demonstrated that the ending of the *Odyssey* is not an excusably lame conclusion and a necessary evil, but an enriching and brilliantly appropriate ending for the great epic, in short, that if Homer didn't write it, the man who wrote it was a Homer.

---

[4] C. M. Bowra, *Tradition and Design in the Iliad* (Oxford, 1930), p. 71.

SELECTED BIBLIOGRAPHY

Allen, T. W. *Homer, the Origins and the Transmission.* Oxford, 1924.

Amory, (Parry) Anne R. *Omens and Dreams in the Odyssey.* Doctoral Dissertation, Radcliffe, 1957.

Armstrong, James I. "The Marriage Song—Od. 23," *Trans. Phil. As.* 89 (1958), 38-43.

Bassett, Samuel Eliot. "The Second Necyia," *CJ* 13 (1918), 521-6.

Bethe, E. "Der Schluss der Odysee und Apollonius von Rhodos," *Hermes* 53 (1918), 444-6.

Bethe, E. "Odysee-Probleme," *Hermes* 63 (1928), 81-92.

Bolling, G. M. *The External Evidence for Interpolation in Homer.* Oxford, 1925.

Bowra, C. M. *Tradition and Design in the Iliad.* Oxford, 1930.

Bury, J. B. "The End of the *Odyssey,*" *JHS* 42 (1922), 1-15.

Calhoun, George H. "Homer's Gods: Prolegomena," *Trans. Phil. As.* 68 (1937), 11-25.

Calhoun, George M. "The Divine Entourage in Homer," *AJP* 61 (1940), 257-277.

Carpenter, Rhys. *Folk Tale, Fiction and Saga in the Homeric Epics,* Berkeley, 1946.

Cauer, Paul. *Grundfragen der Homerkritik.* Leipzig, 1923.

Clarke, Howard W., *The Art of the Odyssey.* Englewood Cliffs, N. J., 1967.

D'Arms, Edward F. and Hulley, Karl K. "The Oresteia-Story in the *Odyssey,*" *Trans. Phil. As.* 77 (1946), 207-13.

Dindorf, Gul., ed., *Scholia Graeca in Homeri Odysseam.* Vol. 1.

Erbse, Hartmut, *Beiträge zum Verstandnis der Odyssee.* Berlin, 1972.

Finley, M. I. *The World of Odysseus,* New York, 1954.

Haymes, Edward R., *A Bibliography of Studies Relating to Parry's and Lord's Oral Theory.* Cambridge, Massachusetts 1973.

Kay, F. L., "Aristarchus' 'τέλος,' *Odyssey* xxiii 296," *CR* 7 (1957), 106.

Kirk, G. S. *The Songs of Homer.* Cambridge, 1962.

Lang, Andrew. *Homer and the Epic.* London, 1893.

Lord, Albert, *The Singer of Tales.* Cambridge, Mass, 1960.

Mackail, J. W. "The Epilogue of the *Odyssey,*" in: *Greek Poetry and Life —Essays presented to Gilbert Murray.* Oxford, 1936, pp. 1-13.

Moulton, Carroll, "The End of the *Odyssey,*" *GRBS* 15, # 2 (1974) 153-169.

Myres, J. L. *Homer and his Critics.* London, 1958.

Myres, J. L. "The Pattern of the Odyssey," *JHS* 72 (1952), 1-19.

Page, Denys, *The Homeric Odyssey.* Oxford, 1955.

Platnauer, M. *Fifty Years of Classical Scholarship.* Oxford, 1954. Articles by E. R. Dodds, L. R. Palmer, and Dorothea Gray.

Pope, Alexander. *The Odyssey of Homer.* London, 1806. Notes, Vol. 6.

Post, L. A. "The Moral Pattern in Homer," *Trans. Phil. As.* 70 (1939), 158-190.

Schlesinger, Alfred C. "The Literary Necessity of Anthropomorphism," *CJ* 32 (1936), 19-26.

Scott, John A. *The Unity of Homer.* Berkeley, 1921.

Scott, John A. *Review of "Die Komp. der Odysee"* by E. Belzner, *CJ* 8, 221.

Scott, John A. "The Close of the *Odyssey,*" *CJ* 12, 397 ff.

Shewan, A. "The 'Continuation' of the *Odyssey,*" in three parts, *CP* 8 (1913), 284-300; *CP* 9 (1914), 35-48; *CP* 9 (1914), 160-173.

Shipp, C. P. *Studies in the Language of Homer*. Cambridge, Mass., 1972.

Spohn, F. A. G. *Commentatio de Extrema Odysseae Parte*. Leipzig. 1816.

Stanford, W. B. "The Ending of the Odyssey: An Ethical Approach," *Hermathena* 100 (1965) 5-20.

Thomson, J. A. K. *Studies in the Odyssey*. Oxford, 1914.

Thornton, Agathe, *People and Themes in Homer's Odyssey*. Dunedin, N.Z. 1970

Van der Valk, Marchinus H. A. L. H. *Textual Criticism of the Odyssey*. Leiden, 1949.

Wace, A. J. B. and Stubbings, Frank H., eds. *A Companion to Homer*. London, 1962.

Wade-Gery, H. T. *The Poet of the Iliad*. Cambridge, 1952.

Whitman, Cedric H. *Homer and the Heroic Tradition*. Cambridge, Mass., 1958.

Wilamowitz-Moellendorff, U. *von. Die Heimkehr des Odysseus*. Berlin, 1927.

Woodhouse, W. J. *The Composition of Homer's Odyssey*. Oxford, 1930.

INDEX OF NAMES

INDEX OF HOMERIC PASSAGES CITED